Historic Houses of the Pacific Northwest

HISTORIC HOUSES OF THE PACIFIC NORTHWEST

DAPHNE REECE

CHRONICLE BOOKS • SAN FRANCISCO

Printed in the United State of America.

LIBRARY OF CONGRESS CATALOGING IN PUBLICATION DATA

Reece, Daphne.
Historic houses of the Pacific Northwest.

1. Historic buildings—Northwest, Pacific—Guide-books.
2. Historic buildings—Alaska—Guide-books. 3. Northwest, Pacific—Description and travel—1981- —Guide-books.
4. Alaska—Description and travel—1981- —Guide-books.
5. Architecture—Northwest, Pacific—Guide-books.
6. Architecture—Alaska—Guide-books. I. Title.
F852.3.R44 1984 917.95 84-21490
ISBN 0-87701-272-5

TYPOGRAPHY Accent & Alphabet, Seattle

CHRONICLE BOOKS
One Hallidie Plaza
San Francisco, CA 94102

PHOTO CREDITS

Aurora Colony Historical Society, Aurora, Oregon, 65; Galen Biery, 99; Blackfoot News, 51; Denise Burke, 114; Chelan County Historical Society Museum, Cashmere, Washington, 102; Clatskanie Senior Citizens, Clatskanie, Oregon, 69; Cleveland and Associates, Seattle, Washington, 141; Cowlitz County Historical Museum, Kelso, Washington, 117; Hermine Duthie, 161; Eastern Washington State Historical Society, Spokane, Washington, 144; Greater Portland Convention and Visitors Association, Portland, Oregon, 85; Historical Architecture Development Corporation, Walla Walla, Washington, 165; Art Hupy Photo, 119; Joe Koontz, 155; Lairmont Manor Trusteeship, Bellingham, Washington, 98; Latah County Historical Society, Moscow, Idaho, 55; Gerry Lewin, 89; Geneva V. Lynch, 77; Matsqui, Sumas, Abbotsford Museum Society, Abbotsford, British Columbia, 11; McLoughlin Memorial Association, Oregon City, Oregon, 83; Archie Miller, 33; Mission Mill Museum, Salem, Oregon, 91; Molalla Area Historical Society, Molalla, Oregon, 80; National Park Service, 7; Charles Neu, 131; Office of Archaeology and Historic Preservation, State of Washington, 105, 121, 123, 127, 135, 137, 139, 143, 147, 153, 157; Oregon Historical Society, Portland, Oregon, 63, 93; Oregon State Society of the Daughters of the American Revolution, 71, 79; Province of British Columbia, 17, 19, 21, 22, 23, 29, 31; Bill Rance, 61; Alice Richards, Driftwood Photo, 27; Sooke Region Museum and Archives, Vancouver Island, Vancouver, British Columbia, 35; Soroptimist International of Vancouver, Inc., 159; Southern Oregon Historical Society, Jacksonville, Oregon, 73; Steilacoom Historical Museum Association, Steilacoom, Washington, 149; Sumner Historical Society, Sumner, Washington, 150; Tourism British Columbia, 13, 15, 25, 36, 37, 39, 40, 41, 42, 43, 44, 46; Walla Walla Valley Pioneer and Historical Society, Walla Walla, Washington, 163; Washington State Parks and Recreation Commission, 103, 109, 125, 133, 167; Mr. and Mrs. Robert Watson, 113.

TABLE OF CONTENTS

FOREWORD

The most striking thing about the Northwest's historic houses is that so many date from the pioneer period. Indeed, the European occupation of the region is so recent that, unlike some parts of the country, evidence of early settlement seems everywhere close at hand. Historic forts and parks, many of them replete with a variety of log structures, do not have to be made up in Disneyland fashion. Instead, the buildings are assembled from nearby sites and, if necessary, complemented with reconstructions. Not only are visitors treated to original structures, often with family histories attached, but orchards and gardens may also remain. In some of the parks, the flavor of the past can literally be tasted in apple cider and fresh-baked bread served by reasonable facsimiles of early settlers. And although purists may argue that such places sanitize the past and serve more to project our own longings than to teach us history's lessons, it is also true that the choice is typically between saving the structures by making them accessible to the public in attractive ways or losing them to the recycling processes of nature or to the bulldozer. The latter also symbolizes historical forces of development at work, but in negative ways that most of us would prefer to avoid. By creating these cameo portraits of the past, we also perpetuate history by giving future historians clues to our own knowledge and understanding.

Early fortunes in lumbering, mining, and railroading produced the mansions that were perceived by their builders to be the rewards for coming so far and enduring so much. Ironically, they had to send back for many of the trappings—carved stairways and panels, stained glass, fancy wall coverings, and so on—which lifted these houses above the homestead level. Only occasionally in the early days were craftsmen present who were equal to the task of creating the ambiance of tradition from scratch.

Though there are fewer extravagances in the Northwest than elsewhere, California for example, there are many, more modest manor houses. Every town seems to have one. They were built by town founders, men and women of affairs, as they used to say, but not necessarily empire builders like the mining and railroading entrepreneurs who resided in the large cities.

Like the empire builders these town people also moved up in the world from log shelters. Often the pioneer cabin remains on the grounds, a chrysalis from which the inhabitants emerged into a newer, brighter world. The contrast between the humble first house and the permanent residence in some newly arrived eastern style must have been more astonishing in the days when the region was less connected to the rest of the country by communication technology. What else explains Hoquiam's calling what, elsewhere, would have been considered simply a generously scaled Queen Anne house, a "Castle"?

Opulent mansions, such as Robert Dunsmuir's Craigdarroch in Victoria; and those of Patrick Clark, Amasa B. Campbell, and James N. Glover in Spokane; and John Leary's and Joshua Green's in Seattle; and Henry Pittock's in Portland fulfill our expectations of how the Northwest's very rich lived in the palmy days. But nothing quite prepares us for the spectral quality of Sam Hill's Maryhill, shimmering like a mirage on the lunar banks of the Columbia River in central Washington. Can it possibly be that Hill originally intended to found an agricultural community here called "The Promised Land"? Or, more unlikely yet, that Queen Marie of Romania dedicated this evocation of an eighteenth-century chateau as a museum "for the betterment of French Art in the Far

Northwest of America"?

This inflation of expectations came naturally to many of the larger-than-life characters whose lives are embodied in their houses. Though we may not get the whole story without the flesh and blood presence, if we stretch our imagination while visiting these houses, humble and grand, we can certainly enlarge our understanding of the role these places have played in creating the Northwest of today. We can also admire the accumulated pride of place which has mobilized energy, concern, and funds to preserve and maintain these houses for our edification.

Sally Woodbridge
Architectural Historian

ALASKA

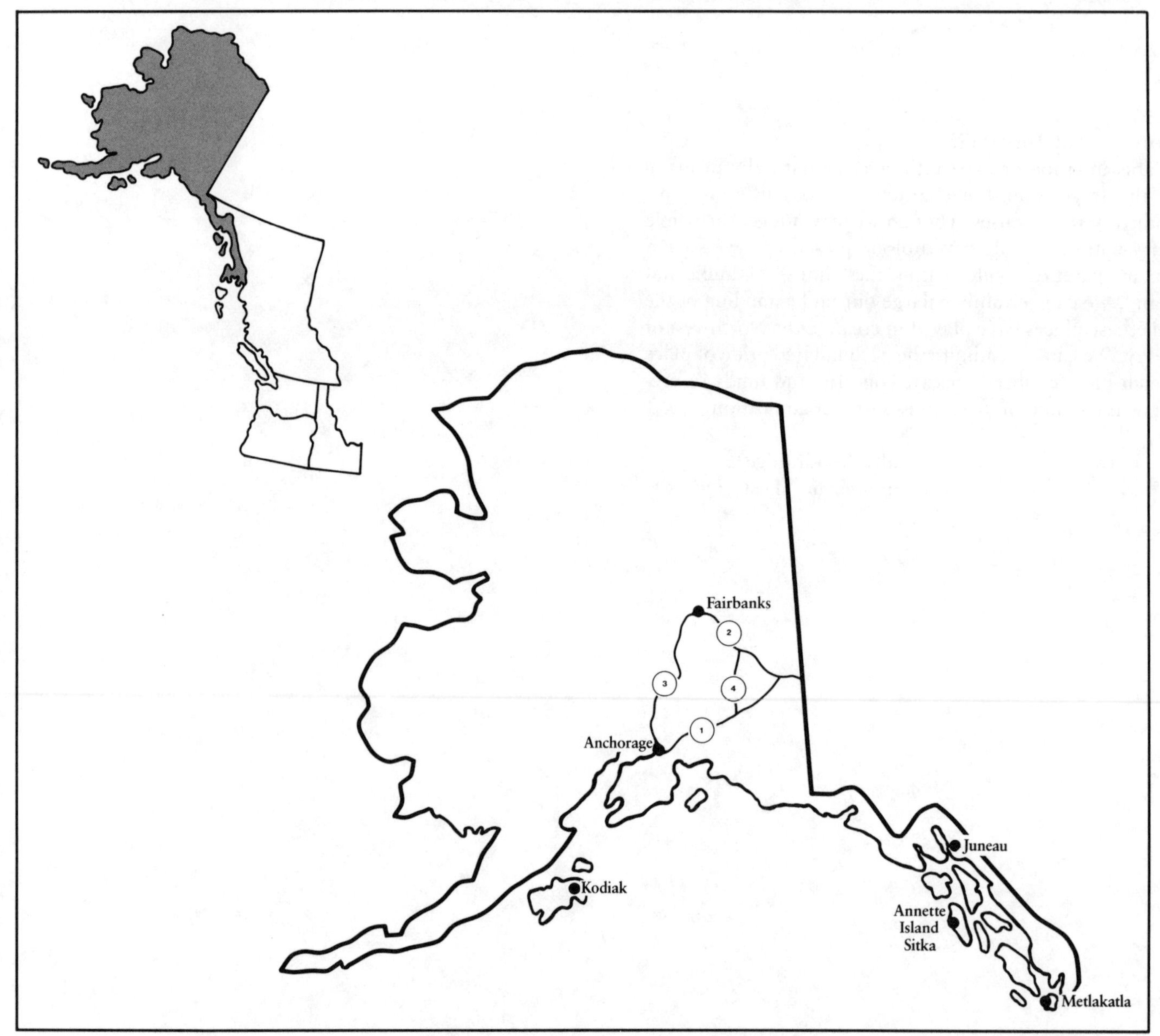

Fairbanks
2
3
4
1
Anchorage
Juneau
Kodiak
Annette
Island
Sitka
Metlakatla

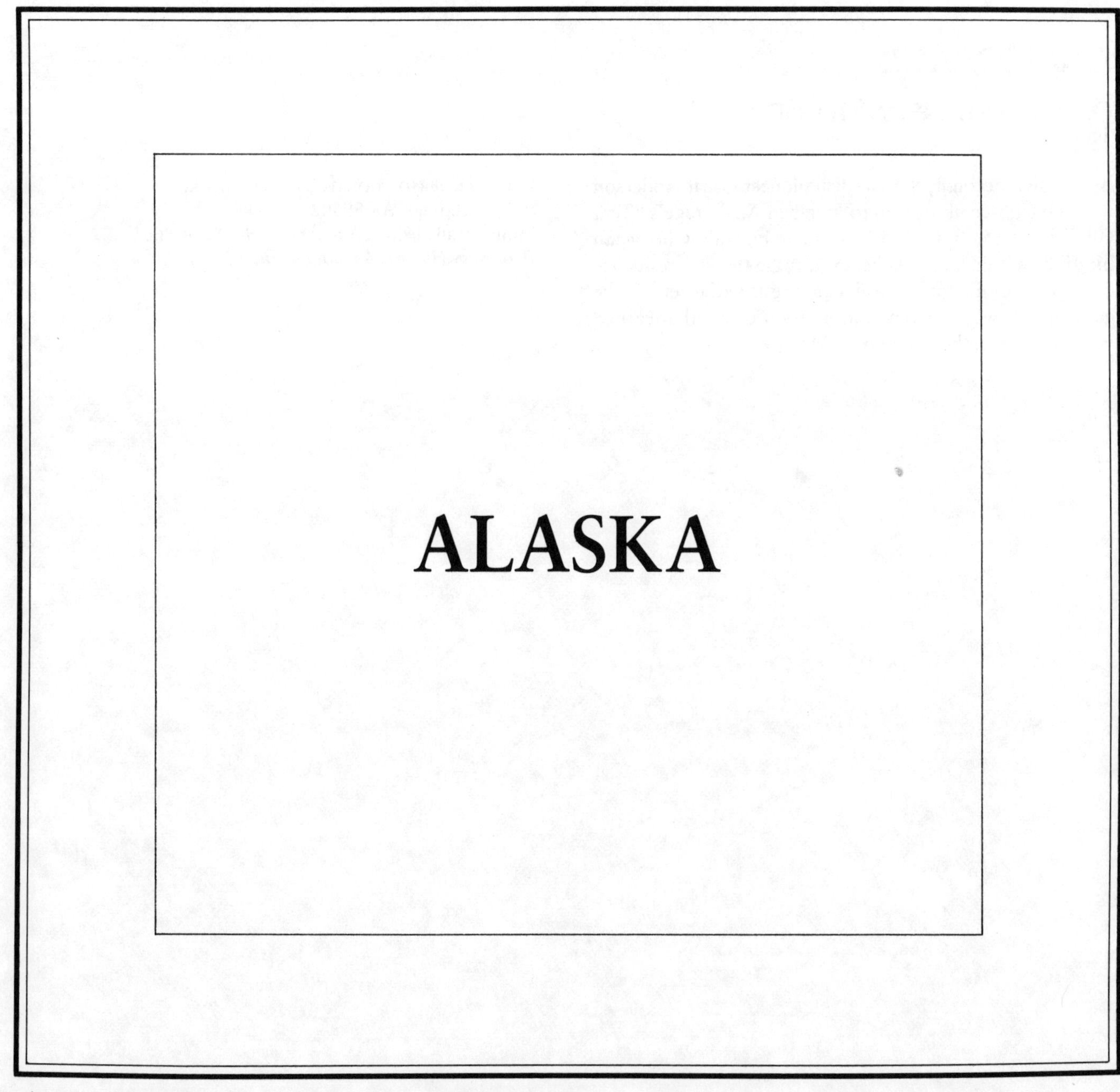

ALASKA

ANCHORAGE

OSCAR ANDERSON HOUSE
1915

By his own account, the Swedish pioneer Oscar Anderson was the eighteenth person to arrive in Anchorage's "Tent City" in 1915, and the simple frame bungalow he began building within weeks is believed to be the first residence completed in the town. Now being restored, it retains the gay yellow, white, green, and maroon colors that earned it its nickname, the Gingerbread House.

OSCAR ANDERSON HOUSE, Elderberry Park,
Anchorage, AK 99502.
Hours: Call Historic Anchorage, (907) 274-9661.
(Courtesy Historic Anchorage, Inc.)

FAIRBANKS

ALASKALAND

Alaska's native and pioneer building traditions are readily explored in this large park on the banks of the Chena River. As one of the attractions of the 1967 Centennial Exposition, some thirty cabins and buildings constructed during Fairbanks's early days were brought here to create Gold Rush Town, an evocation of the stampede era, complete with boardwalks and signs. At Alaska Kha Yah, a little farther east of Gold Rush Town, architects and native craftsmen have replicated authentic nineteenth-century houses and outbuildings of the Alaskan Eskimo and Athabascan Indians. Among them are a King Island house, Ingalik and St. Michael kashims, and a spruce plank house. Alaskan artifacts are for sale in the kashims.

Gold Rush Town

The classic pioneer cabin of Alaska's early days was from 12 to 16 feet wide and 16 to 20 feet long, constructed of peeled logs, with a low-pitched overhanging gable roof that sheltered a small door and a large window at the front. Several of these veterans front the boardwalk of Alaskaland's Sourdough Way. One of the oldest, cabin 14, built before 1904 by two Finns, still retains its original mud chinking and adjacent cache where furs, supplies, and survival gear were stored secure from prowling animals.

The *Kitty Hensley House* (early 1900s) is a fanciful variation of the basic cabin. Originally just two small rooms and a lean-to shed, the cabin was enlarged in 1914 with the addition of a second story, a hip roof, patterned shingling, and a Palladian window in the front facade. Hensley House, now used as a museum of pioneer life in Fairbanks, houses antiques and memorabilia.

Across the street is *Wickersham House* (1904), built by the celebrated Judge James Wickersham (see House of Wickersham, Juneau). This single-story frame house is believed to be the first home in Fairbanks to be built of milled lumber.

The *Loomis Cabin,* a two-story house with leaded windows, was built in 1903 by Lee B. Loomis, founder of Loomis Security, who first came to Alaska in the gold rush of 1897. Loomis soon found that providing supplies to miners was a surer road to wealth than grubbing for pay dirt. In those early years he realized the need for a safe way to transport money and valuables, but it was not until the 1920s that he began the armored car service that still bears his name.

In the outskirts of Gold Rush Town, opposite the railway station, is the last home of one of Alaska's most versatile pioneers. Harry Karstens was a youth of seventeen when he came to the Klondike in 1897; to earn his expenses for the trip he had backpacked supplies over the Chilkoot Pass. He became "the best outdoors man and dog musher in the North," helped lay out the townsite of Eagle on the Yukon River, and with his partner Charlie McGonagall blazed the first trail by dog team from Fairbanks to Valdez to deliver the mail. He was also a miner, a broker, a riverboat operator, and even a bill collector. But he is best remembered as the conqueror of Mt. McKinley, the highest mountain in the United States, whose northeast ridge is now known as Karstens' Ridge.

ALASKALAND, Airport Way and Peger Road,
Fairbanks, AK 99701; (907) 452-4529.
Hours: Posted seasonally. Call (907) 452-4529.
(Courtesy Fairbanks Convention and Visitors Bureau)

JUNEAU

HOUSE OF WICKERSHAM
1899

The House of Wickersham was the home of one of Alaska's most distinguished pioneers. James Wickersham, historian, congressman, and pioneer judge, came to Alaska in 1900 to investigate the great gold scandal at Nome and to establish the first courts and government in the interior. As congressman he secured the state's first territorial legislature and home rule; he also introduced the legislation that established Mt. McKinley National Park, the University of Alaska, and the building of the Alaska Railroad. He named the city of Fairbanks and led the first attempt to climb Mt. McKinley. His home preserves his extensive collection of artifacts dating from the Russian-American period, and many personal mementoes. It is still a private residence—the home of Mrs. Ruth Allman, the judge's niece, who hosts visitors to traditional "flaming sourdough" waffles (the sourdough pot was started over sixty years ago).

HOUSE OF WICKERSHAM, 213 Seventh Avenue, Juneau, AK 99801; (907) 586-1251.

Hours: Open daily, May 28–September 30. Tours at 1:30 and 6:30. Reservations must be made through Alaska Exploration Holidays, Juneau; (907) 586-1251. Special tours may be arranged for groups of more than 12 persons.

Admission fee.

(Courtesy Mrs. Ruth Allman and Byron Fish)

KODIAK

BARANOF-ERSKINE HOUSE
Ca. 1792; altered 1870 and 1912

For all its up-to-date exterior, the Baranof-Erskine House is one of the oldest buildings on the Pacific Coast. Constructed with Aleut labor sometime between 1792 and 1793, it served as a fur warehouse and the manager's office when Alexander Baranof directed the affairs of the Russian American Company from the 1790s to 1819. In the 1870s, red cedar was brought up from California to sheath the log timbers of the original structure, and around 1880 the originally hipped roof was given gables. In 1911 the building was purchased by W. J. Erskine, who altered the building for use as his family residence. It now serves as a museum of the Kodiak Island group.

BARANOF-ERSKINE HOUSE (Baranof Museum), Center Street and Marine Way, Kodiak, AK 99615; (907) 485-5920.
Hours: Summer, 10–3 Monday–Friday, 12–4 Saturday and Sunday; winter, 11–3 Tuesday–Friday, 1–4 Saturday and Sunday.
Admission fee.
(Courtesy Kodiak Historical Society)

METLAKATLA (ANNETTE ISLAND)

FATHER WILLIAM DUNCAN COTTAGE 1894

This simple cabin was the home of Father William Duncan, the spiritual, social, and economic leader of the Metlakatla Indian community during its formative years. A Scot, Duncan arrived in Fort Simpson, British Columbia, in 1857 to serve as a lay minister to the Tsimshian Indians of Old Metlakatla. He learned their language and succeeded in establishing a prosperous model community. Duncan could tolerate no interference, however, and when controversy arose with the Anglican church over religious affairs, he moved the community from Canada to unoccupied Annette Island, Alaska. He dedicated the settlement "New Metlakatla" on August 7, 1887. In 1891 the U.S. Congress granted the Metlakatla Indians title to the entire island, the first land grant reservation in the territory. Duncan's home, restored as a museum, contains many of his personal possessions.

FATHER WILLIAM DUNCAN COTTAGE, Metlakatla, Annette Island, AK 99926; (907) 886-5926.

Hours: Summer, 8–5 Monday–Friday; winter, 9–5 Monday–Friday. Open weekends by request.

(Courtesy Metlakatla Indian Community Tribal Community Services)

SITKA

SITKA NATIONAL HISTORICAL PARK
RUSSIAN BISHOP'S HOUSE
1842–43

Roofed in iron, this weathered two-story structure of squared spruce logs was built by the Russian American Company for the use of the bishop of New Archangel (New Archangel was the former name of Sitka). When restoration is completed, the second story will depict the bishop's living quarters and chapel as they appeared between 1843 and 1853. Several of the items of furniture displayed were probably made by the first resident bishop, Bishop Innocent, later metropolitan of Moscow.

RUSSIAN BISHOP'S HOUSE, Sitka National Historical Park, Sitka, AK 99835; (907) 747-6281.
Hours: Posted on a seasonal basis.
(Courtesy National Park Service)

BRITISH COLUMBIA

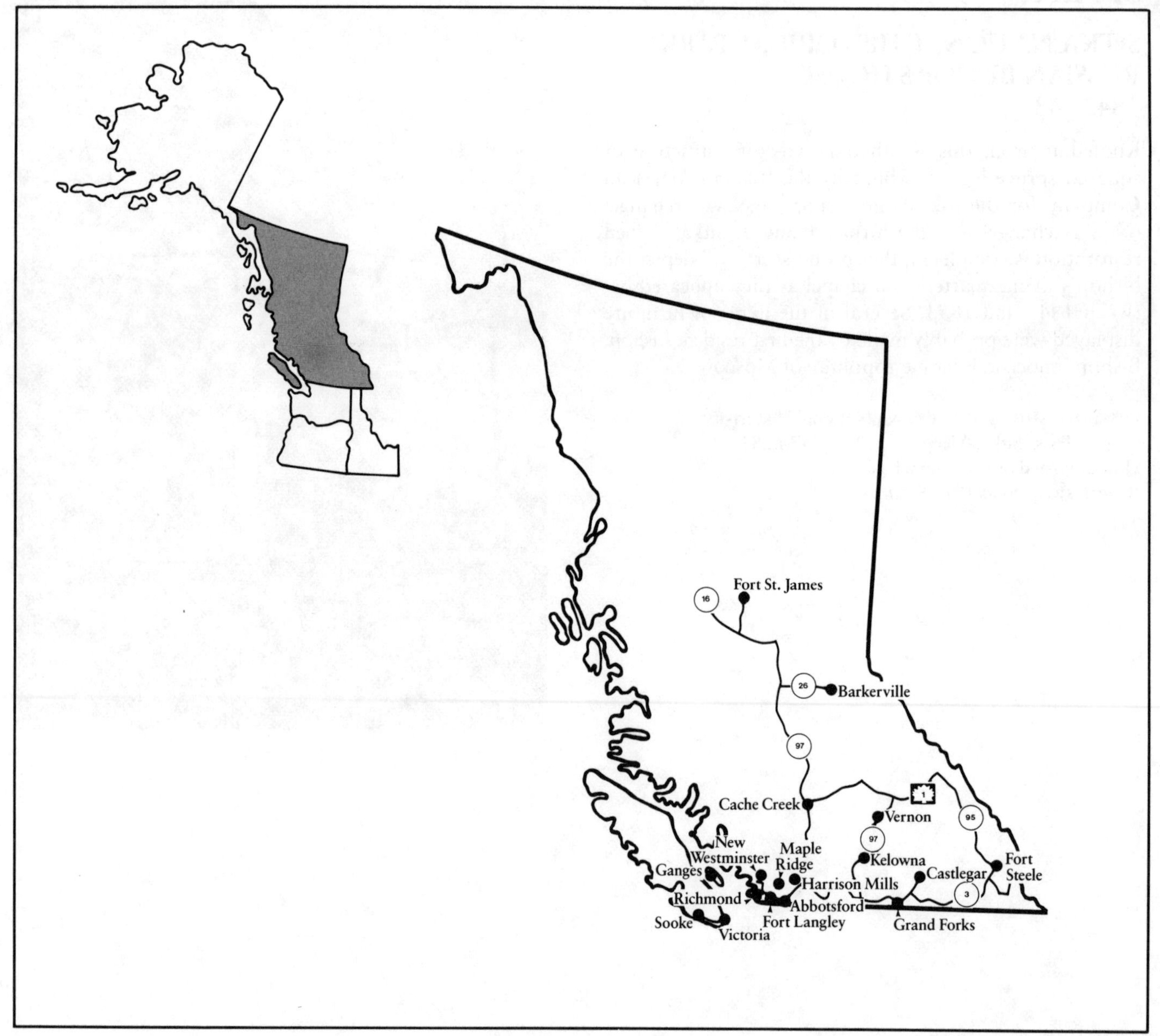

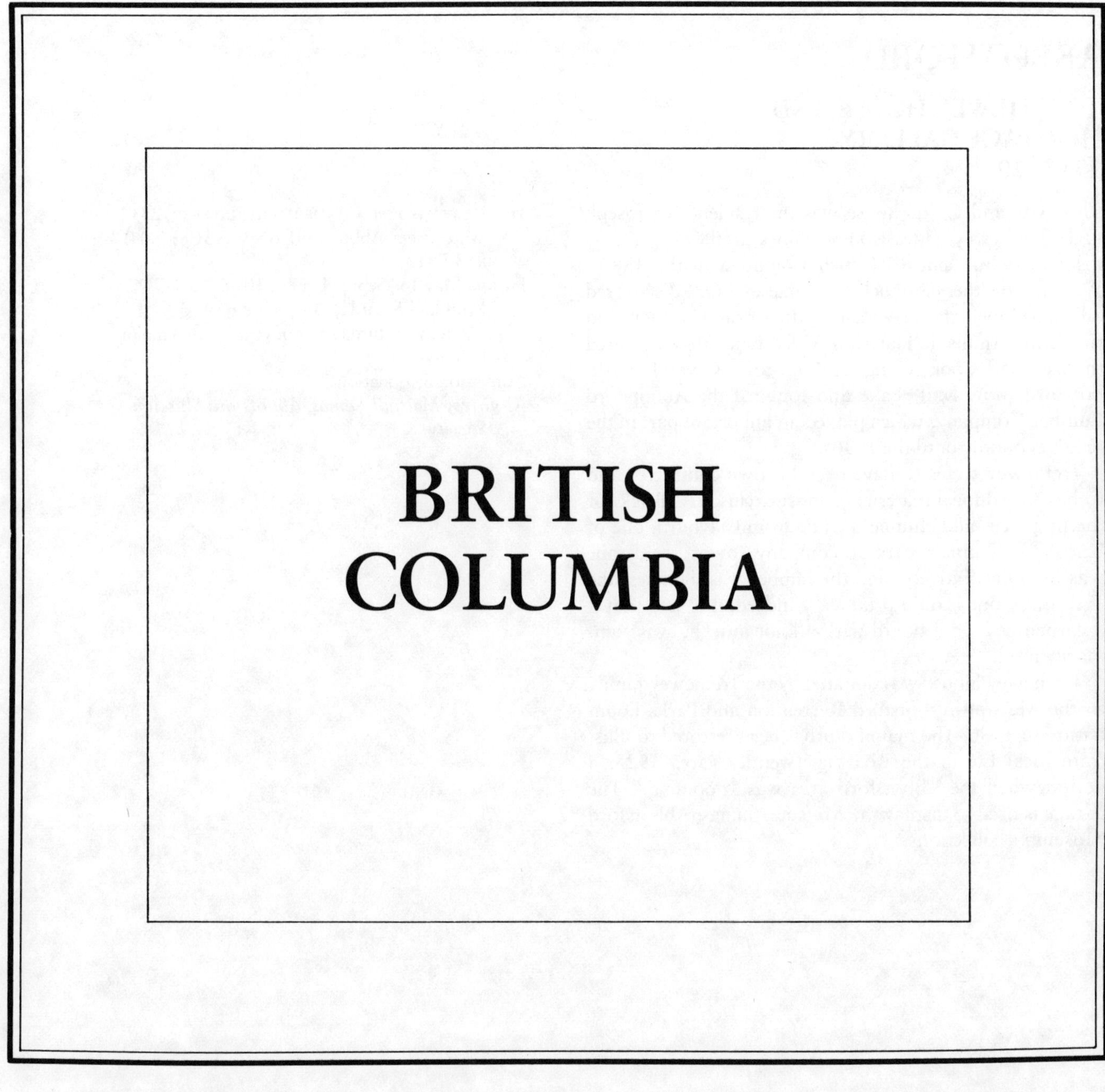

BRITISH COLUMBIA

ABBOTSFORD

TRETHEWEY HOUSE AND HERITAGE GALLERY 1917–20

This Arts and Crafts house was the residence of Joseph Ogle Trethewey, eldest son of James Trethewey, a Cornishman who came to British Columbia in the 1860s. With his brothers Samuel and James, "J.O." discovered and developed the Providence Mine near Harrison and the lumber mills at Harrison Mills. Later they acquired the assets of Cook, Craig, & Johnston's sawmill at Abbotsford (now Mill) Lake and founded the Abbotsford Lumber Company, which played an important part in the area's economy until the 1930s.

Trethewey seems to have been his own contractor and to have used local materials almost exclusively. Brick for the fireplaces and chimneys came from Clayburn, one of British Columbia's earliest company towns; fieldstone was used decoratively; and the lumber was the finest the Trethewey mills could produce—indeed, it is said that if a carpenter used a board with a knot in it, he was summarily fired.

Trethewey House was donated by the Trethewey family to the Matsqui-Abbotsford Recreation and Parks Foundation in 1980. The main floor has been restored to illustrate local life in the Roaring Twenties, circa 1925, a period when the Abbotsford area was "booming." The garage is used to display the Matsqui, Sumas, Abbotsford Museum's collections.

TRETHEWEY HOUSE AND HERITAGE GALLERY, 2313 Ware Street, Abbotsford, BC V2S 3C6; (604) 853-0313

Hours: May 15–September 16, 10–8 Monday–Saturday, 1–8 Sunday; 1–5 Monday–Saturday rest of year. Closed major holidays.

Admission by donation.

(Courtesy Matsqui, Sumas, Abbotsford Museum Society)

BARKERVILLE

BARKERVILLE PROVINCIAL HISTORIC PARK 1868–85

The excitement and vitality of the Cariboo Gold Rush have returned to Barkerville. When in 1958 the province of British Columbia decided to restore the town as a historic park, little remained of early Barkerville. The log shanties, false-fronted stores and saloons that had sprung up around the claim where Billy Barker gleaned a thousand dollars worth of nuggets in forty-eight hours were long gone, wiped out by a fire that razed most of the town in just over two hours on September 16, 1868. And although Barkerville was then rebuilt within six weeks and continued to thrive until the turn of the century, the flood of gold seekers ebbed away, lured by dreams of easier wealth in the Stikine and Omineca fields. With the rise of Wells as the center of hard rock mining in the 1930s, Barkerville became virtually a ghost town.

Restoration has created a living museum of some one hundred original and reconstructed buildings that draw you into every aspect of "boom town" life of the 1870s. Most of them were constructed between 1868 and 1900 and include many that belonged to Barkerville's large Chinese community. But before you set off down the boardwalks, it's a good idea to visit the park museum, where displays and audiovisual presentations provide excellent background information. Entertainments have also caught the spirit of the era. There are shows at the Theatre Royal like those the miners enjoyed over a century ago, and a dramatic presentation of Judge Matthew Begbie's colorful career may be seen at Richfield Courthouse. Traditional Cariboo mining fare is served at the historic Wake-Up Jake Cafe. At the Eldorado Mine you can try your luck at gold panning, then spend your "poke" on late Victorian goods at Mason & Daly's general store, and count what's left over a cool root beer in the original Barkerville Hotel built in 1869. Perhaps you'll hear the clink of glasses and the ghostly laughter of the hurdy gurdy girls who charged the miners a dollar for a dance.

BARKERVILLE PROVINCIAL HISTORIC PARK, Barkerville, BC V0K 1B0; (604) 994-3209. Located 55 miles east of Quesnel on Highway 26.
Hours: Open daily, May–September, 8–8; rest of year 9–4. Museum and Theatre Royal open summer only; special events July 1–Labor Day.
No general admission fee. Rates for special events such as Theatre Royal and gold panning.
(Courtesy Province of British Columbia Ministry of Lands, Parks and Housing, Parks and Outdoor Recreation Division)

BARKERVILLE

COTTONWOOD HOUSE PROVINCIAL HISTORIC PARK
1864–65

After John Boyd acquired Cottonwood House in March 1874, word soon spread among travelers plying the old Cariboo Wagon Road that the roadhouse between Barkerville and Quesnel was now in the best of hands. A weary freighter driving into the breezeway of the large double barn knew that his stock would be fed on Timothy and oat hay grown on the property, and that he could count on a wholesome meal in the dining room before retiring to a clean bed in either a dormitory or a private room. He could, too, if necessary, send a telegram from the Overland Telegraph office established at Cottonwood in 1868, leave messages in care of the Boyds, and replenish his supplies at the general store they operated in the storehouse. The Boyds also boarded horses and mules and added a guest house in 1883 for visitors who wished to stay for an extended period of time.

The family operated the roadhouse continuously for seventy-seven years, until the fall of 1951. In 1963 the provincial government acquired eleven of the original fifty-nine hectares, including Cottonwood House and the major outbuildings, to establish a historic park. Displays in the Interpretation Center provide useful background information on Cottonwood House, one of the oldest buildings in British Columbia. Stagecoach rides through the park add to the fun.

COTTONWOOD HOUSE PROVINCIAL HISTORIC PARK, R.R. 4, Cottonwood No. 18, Quesnel, BC V2J 3H8; (604) 992-9598. Located 18 miles east of Quesnel on Highway 26.

Hours: Open daily May 15–September 30, 8 A.M. to dusk.

(Courtesy Province of British Columbia, Ministry of Lands, Parks and Housing, Parks and Outdoor Recreation Division)

CACHE CREEK

HAT CREEK HOUSE
Pre-1912

Hat Creek House *may* be the oldest roadhouse on the Old Cariboo Trail: the origins of this two-story Red River frame house still puzzle the historian and the archaeologist. There's good evidence that George Dunne erected two buildings after acquiring the property in 1866; and when Donald Maclean, a former Hudson's Bay Company fur trader homesteaded in the area between 1860 and 1864, early gazettes noted "Maclean's farm and restaurant." Certainly the inner core of the house is a square, single-story log structure built in the Hudson's Bay Company construction style. It may be that this log core was moved to the property from another company site. The addition of a second story in 1880 was the first of many alterations over the years as the house changed hands. From 1905 until 1911 it was operated as a roadhouse; thereafter it served as the residence of Charles Doering, one-time owner of the Vancouver Breweries until its purchase by the British Columbia Heritage Trust in 1952.

Hat Creek House today is a historic site in the making. There's an extensive wagon and agricultural machinery collection, and when restoration is completed, the former way station for travelers on the Cariboo Road will depict the agriculture, transportation, and tourism of early British Columbia.

HAT CREEK HOUSE, Old Cariboo Trail, Cache Creek, BC V0K 1H0.
Hours: For information, call Hat Creek House Restoration Society, P.O. Box 159, Cache Creek, BC V0K 1H0; (604) 453-2458.
(Courtesy Province of British Columbia, Heritage Conservation Branch, and Hat Creek House Restoration Society)

CASTLEGAR

DOUKHOBOR HISTORICAL VILLAGE

Here in the heartland of the Doukhobor settlements of Western Canada, the Kootenay Doukhobor Historical Society has constructed a replica of a Doukhobor communal village, commemorating the beliefs and way of life of a Christian sect that originated in eighteenth-century Russia. Spiritual kin of the Quakers and the Amish in their rejection of religious formalism and governmental authority, their pacifism, and their ideal of a simple agrarian society, the Doukhobors came to Canada from the Crimea in 1899 to settle lands in Saskatchewan set aside for them under the Homestead Act. But many Doukhobors, averse to governmental restraints and what they regarded as the corrupting influence of their neighbors, moved to British Columbia in 1908. In the valleys of the southern interior they established some ninety communal villages, each housing about a hundred people, where they developed a self-sufficient economy based on a reverent and cherishing attitude toward the soil.

Doukhobor Historical Village suggests the lifestyle of the period 1900 to the late 1930s with a characteristic pair of large brick houses surrounded by an orchard, gardens, and agricultural outbuildings. There is a rich array of handcrafted farm and household objects on display, a restaurant offering traditional Doukhobor food, and in the adjacent National Exhibition Centre and Castlegar Museum a variety of different shows is offered year round. Doukhobor cottage crafts are for sale in the Cultural Education Centre. Do not miss an opportunity to hear the haunting sounds of a Doukhobor choir.

DOUKHOBOR HISTORICAL VILLAGE, P.O. Box 3081, Castlegar, BC V1N 3H4; (604) 365-6622. Located opposite Castlegar Airport.

Hours: June–August, 8–8 daily; rest of year, 9–5 daily.

Admission fee.

(Courtesy Kootenay Doukhobor Historical Society)

FORT LANGLEY

FORT LANGLEY NATIONAL HISTORIC PARK 1827

Fort Langley was established near the mouth of the Fraser River in 1827 by George Simpson, governor of the Hudson's Bay Company, as part of his plan to end American competition in the lucrative fur trade. Under the direction of Chief Trader Archibald McDonald, Fort Langley did indeed dominate trade with the Indians of Puget Sound, Vancouver Island, and the Fraser River until the supply of animals in its immediate area became exhausted. The fort's primary function then shifted to provisioning. Its farm and fishery operations supplied many of the basic needs of the Company's ships and of its trading posts, which by the 1850s extended deep into the interior. When gold was discovered on the upper reaches of the Fraser in 1858 and thirty thousand prospectors poured into the area within two months, the fort was able to supply their needs.

The Fort Langley you visit today is a reconstruction, located on the site chosen in 1839 to be closer to its important farming operations. That post was destroyed by fire the same year, and of the new buildings put up in 1840 only the storehouse remains. It has been refurbished as a Hudson's Bay Company store of the fur trade era, even to pelts hung on the walls. The four reconstructed buildings include the "Big House" where, on a gray November morning in 1858, a hundred people gathered in the hall to hear the proclamation establishing British government of the Pacific mainland. Costumed personnel give meaning to the displays with demonstrations of pioneer working methods in the 1840s and 1850s.

FORT LANGLEY NATIONAL HISTORIC PARK, P.O. Box 129, Mavis Street, Fort Langley, BC V0X 1J0; (604) 888-4424.
Hours: Open daily, June 16–Labor Day, 10–6; rest of year, 10–4:30. Closed major holidays.
Admission fee.
(Courtesy Parks Canada)

FORT ST. JAMES

FORT ST. JAMES NATIONAL HISTORIC PARK
1806; restored to mid-1890s

Fort St. James National Historic Park is located in the second-oldest settlement in British Columbia. After establishing a fur-trading post for the North West Company at MacLeod Lake in 1806, Simon Fraser pressed deeper into the Carrier Indian country in his search for a navigable route to the Pacific. He built the first Fort St. James here on the shores of Stuart Lake that same year. Throughout its history the fort served as headquarters of the New Caledonia district, which, after the Hudson's Bay and North West companies merged in 1821, came to include almost all of central British Columbia. So harsh were the winters and so isolated the life here that during the nineteenth century employees regarded service at Fort St. James as a form of punishment.

Five of the buildings you see today date from the period 1884–89. The *General Warehouse and Fur Store* (1888–89), regarded as one of the finest Red River frame buildings still standing in Canada, housed the fort's trade goods and furs. The *Men's House* (1884) served as a residence for company employees, pack train hands, boat crews, and visitors. It was later used as a schoolhouse and as a private residence. The *Officer's Dwelling House* (1882–84) was the home of the manager in charge of the fort. It has been restored to the year 1896. The *Dairy* was used as a storage building for milk and cheese and as a general service building for the main house. The *Fish Cache* (1889), stocked with dried salmon, is an adaptation of the traditional Carrier Indian fish cache. Other structures in the park are accurate reconstructions.

FORT ST. JAMES NATIONAL HISTORIC PARK, P.O. Box 1148, Highway 27, Fort St. James, BC V0J 1P0; (604) 996-7191.
Hours: May 14–October 8, 9–6 daily; rest of year, 8–4:30 Monday–Friday. Closed major holidays. Tours available by reservation.
Admission fee.
(Courtesy Parks Canada)

FORT STEELE

FORT STEELE PROVINCIAL HISTORIC PARK

The story of old Fort Steele, site of this provincial historic park, goes back to the 1864 Kootenay gold rush. Rather than gamble on a fortune in White Horse Creek's rich placer diggings, John Galbraith began a profitable ferry service across the Kootenay River. During the gold years the little community of Galbraith's Ferry that grew up near the crossing became the center of economic and social life in the East Kootenays. The first North West Mounted Police post in British Columbia was established there in 1887 in response to the threat of Indian uprisings; to honor its commander, Samuel B. Steele, who restored peaceful relations without firing a shot, the residents changed the town's name to Fort Steele. But the good times began to wane in 1898 when the new railroad bypassed the town in favor of nearby Cranbrook, and after 1905 Fort Steele became a ghost town.

Fort Steele Provincial Historic Park shows how people worked and lived in the East Kootenay region between 1890 and 1905. Restored buildings from old Fort Steele stand alongside structures moved here from other locations. In summer a varied activities program recaptures the turn of the century with stage shows at the Wild Horse Theatre, stagecoach and steam locomotive rides, and demonstrations of pioneer crafts. For the enthusiast of vernacular architecture there are more than forty buildings to admire.

The *Anglican Vicarage* (1898), with its ornate porch and decorative crestings on the roof ridge, is considered the best example of a Victorian house in Fort Steele. *Cohn House* (1890s) is used for interpretation programs about turn-of-the-century life. *Mather House* (ca. 1893), a plain two-story home with a gabled roof, belonged to Robert Duncan Mather, who imported long-haired cattle from Scotland and started a ranch at Cherry; he also operated a pack train service, opened one of the first sawmills in the area, and built the Dalgardno Hotel (now the Windsor). *Hanson House* (1897–1900), *Taenhauser House,* and *Wolf Creek Cabin* (ca. 1864) keep their origins and stories to themselves. Between Main Street and the river are the surviving and reconstructed buildings of the *North West Mounted Police Post.*

FORT STEELE PROVINCIAL HISTORIC PARK, Fort Steele, BC V0B 1N0; (604) 489-3351. Ten miles northeast of Cranbrook on Highway 93/95.

Hours: Park, Heritage Museum, open daily year round, dawn to dusk. Museum, Kershaw General Store & Tea Room, May–October, 10–5; June–September, 10–6; July–August, 9–8. The museum is open on request November 1–April 30.

(Courtesy Province of British Columbia, Ministry of Lands, Parks and Housing, Parks and Outdoor Recreation Division)

GANGES (SALT SPRING ISLAND)

BITTANCOURT HERITAGE HOUSE MUSEUM 1884

Should you make your way to Salt Spring Island in the Strait of Georgia and wonder about island history, you can learn a good deal by visiting this little frame house in Ganges that contains memorabilia of the early settlers, photographs, and artifacts of the local Indians.

Bittancourt Heritage House itself is part of the pioneer history of the place. It was built by Estalon Jose Bittancourt, a Portuguese who came to Salt Spring Island in about 1858, as the annex to his Vesuvius Bay hotel and was later used as his home. Bittancourt and his wife raised two sons and six daughters in this house; later it was occupied by their son Fred. After the Salt Spring Island Farmers' Institute purchased the house in 1980, it was moved to Ganges, renovated, and restored to serve as the island's museum.

The Bittancourts left behind them four other buildings that still stand in the Vesuvius Bay area: a small Catholic chapel built in 1898 or 1899, known as "The Ark," and three dowry houses that Estalon built for three of his daughters.

BITTANCOURT HERITAGE HOUSE MUSEUM, 351 Rainbow Road, Ganges, Salt Spring Island, BC V0S 1E0; (604) 537-4214.
Hours: Summer only, 11–4 Saturday, Sunday, and holiday Mondays.
(Courtesy Bittancourt Heritage House Museum)

GRAND FORKS

MOUNTAIN VIEW DOUKHOBOR MUSEUM 1912

On the slopes of Hardy Mountain, commanding a panoramic view of Sunshine Valley and the city of Grand Forks, is an attractive two-story house of weathered red brick, its porch shaded by a tumbling screen of wisteria. Mountain View Doukhobor Museum, the home of two branches of the Makortoff family until 1971, is typical of the many communal houses constructed by the Doukhobors in southern British Columbia during the early years of this century. Its plan and architectural style follow the dicta of the Doukhobor leader, Peter V. "Lordly" Verigin. Its bricks, lumber, furniture, and furnishings were all of Doukhobor manufacture. Two such houses and their outbuildings could constitute a communal village for as many as a hundred people.

The house was purchased from the Makortoffs by Peter M. Gritchen in 1971 and has been developed by him as a historic site. Rare and beautiful examples of Doukhobor handicrafts are prominent in an extensive collection of artifacts that includes personal belongings of Peter Verigin and photographs illustrating the lifestyle of the Doukhobor communal period.

MOUNTAIN VIEW DOUKHOBOR MUSEUM, P.O. Box 1235/Hardy Mountain Road, Grand Forks, BC V0H 1H0; (604) 442-8855.

Open for viewing June–September. Call for hours. Admission fee.

(Courtesy Peter M. Gritchen)

HARRISON MILLS

KILBY PROVINCIAL HISTORIC PARK 1904

Thomas Kilby's turn-of-the-century General Store and Hotel—all that is now vital of the logging community of Harrison Mouth, established in the 1870s—is the core of this unusual historic park that portrays and interprets the role of the general store in British Columbia life. It is a large wooden building, three stories high and set on stilts above the flood plain, with the false front, balcony, gabled roof, and shiplap sheathing typical of the "Boomtown Commercial" style. Behind it is the Kilby home. Thomas used the first two floors for his store; the third served as a hotel until 1910, when traffic across the Harrison River fell off with the completion of the railway to Chilliwack. He then rented the rooms to local workers for some years. The store continued in operation until 1977 under Thomas and later his son Acton, although the community it served slipped into oblivion soon after the burning of the lumber mills in 1930.

Today Kilby's General Store is a museum furnished to the period between the two world wars. There's an extensive collection of products, product containers, advertising materials, and store fixtures that appeal as much to those who find them quaint as to those who shopped before the supermarket age. The rooms are unaltered; those on the third floor are furnished as a rural hostelry typical of British Columbia's early years. Across the meadow where the Kilbys pastured their prize Jerseys there is a campground-picnic site on the banks of the Harrison River.

KILBY PROVINCIAL HISTORIC PARK, P.O. Box 48/ 215 Kilby Road, Harrison Mills, BC V0M 1L0; (604) 796-9576. To get there, turn south from Highway 7 at the east end of the Harrison River Bridge and follow the country road for one mile. The turnoff is approximately 23 miles east of Mission City.

Hours: May 15–Labor Day, 10–4 daily; Labor Day–mid-November, 10–4 Thursday–Monday; mid-November–mid-March, 10–4 Saturday and Sunday; mid-March–mid-May, 10–4 Thursday–Monday.

(Courtesy Province of British Columbia, Ministry of Lands, Parks and Housing, Parks and Outdoor Recreation Division)

KELOWNA

FATHER PANDOSY MISSION 1860

It was in October 1859 that Fathers Charles Pandosy and Pierre Richard of the Oblate Order, veterans of missionary work in the northwestern United States and Esquimault, British Columbia, arrived in the Okanagan Valley to establish a new mission. They camped beside Duck Lake for the winter, moved to Dry Creek the following spring, and began construction of mission buildings the same year on the banks of what became known as Mission Creek. Until the Oblates left the Kelowna area in 1908, the mission played an important part in the development of the valley. Here were the first non-Indian settlement, the first school, the first church, and the first agricultural development. The apple trees planted by the fathers were the basis of the great fruit industry that now flourishes in the Okanagan Valley.

By the 1950s few of the original buildings remained. Three have been restored and supplemented by several other historic structures brought in from the surrounding area.

Father Pandosy lies in an unmarked grave on the mission grounds. Born to a landowning family near Marseilles, France, in 1824, he was by all accounts a huge man of unusual strength, and with a booming voice, a ready wit and a nice sense of the *beau geste*. The story is told that one evening while he first camped at Duck Lake, he found himself surrounded by hostile Indians. Coolly he picked up a butcher's knife, walked to a nearby tree, and cut a small circle in the bark. Then he paced off several steps, turned and hurled the knife dead center. By the third demonstration of his skill, the Indians had vanished.

Father Pandosy spent the rest of his life in the Okanagan Valley, ministering to settlers and Indians alike. He died in 1891.

FATHER PANDOSY MISSION, R.R. 4/Benvoulin Road, Kelowna, BC V1Y 6S4.
Hours: April–October, 9–5 daily. Student guides are present in July and August.
Voluntary donations appreciated.
(Courtesy Okanagan Historical Society)

MAPLE RIDGE

HANEY HOUSE
1878

Haney House, built in 1878 for Thomas and Annie Haney, remained the residence of their descendants until 1979, when it was bequeathed to the municipality of Maple Ridge and restored to display furnishings and artifacts of three generations of the Haney family.

Thomas Haney grew up in Ontario and came west in 1876 by way of the California goldfields. Looking for better business opportunities he sailed to British Columbia, where he purchased 160 acres of the Wickwire estate in Maple Ridge for $1,000. Public spirited and energetic, he became a municipal councilor and assessor, laid out the townsite of Port Haney in 1882, and established the first waterworks system in the town. Both the Haneys were devout Roman Catholics, and until 1881, when the first Catholic church was built, services were held in their home.

The original two-story frame farmhouse was patterned after a limestone and wrought-iron home built by Haney's brother in Ontario, though the economic and social differences between eastern and western Canada at that time dictated a simpler structure.

HANEY HOUSE, 11612 224th Street, Maple Ridge, BC V2X 5Z7; (604) 467-1880.
Hours: 1–4 Wednesday and Sunday.
Donations accepted.
(Courtesy Haney House, Municipality of Maple Ridge)

NEW WESTMINSTER

IRVING HOUSE HISTORIC CENTRE 1862–64

Members of the Royal Engineers under private contract built this Gothic Revival house with ornate bargeboards for Capt. William Irving, son of a shipwright in Annan, Dumfriesshire, who pioneered the riverboat trade of the lower Fraser River. A successful "blue water" mariner from the day in 1831 that he signed on aboard the brig *Helen Douglas* bound for Boston until his marriage in Portland, Oregon, in 1851, Irving was alert to the potential of the West's coastal lumber trade and of the steam engine. He brought the first steamboat, the little iron *Eagle,* to the Pacific Northwest in 1851, providing regular service on the Willamette River between Oregon City and Portland. Eight years later he took his family to Victoria and introduced the stern-wheeler to the Fraser. So successful were his ventures that Irving eventually gained a virtual monopoly of New Westminster's shipping business.

His home on a bluff above the river has been a historic center since the city of New Westminster purchased it from his descendants in 1950. There are fourteen rooms, with floors laid and caulked like a ship's deck, marble fireplaces, and ornate plasterwork, and all are furnished to illustrate life in the period 1864–90. Two rooms—the parlor and the bedroom—contain original furniture used by the Irvings. Directly behind the house is the New Westminster Museum, with displays of local history and memorabilia.

IRVING HOUSE HISTORIC CENTRE, 302 Royal Avenue, New Westminster, BC V3L 1H7; (604) 521-7656.
Hours: May 1–mid-September, 11–5 Tuesday–Sunday; mid-September–April 30, 1–5 Saturday and Sunday.
Donations appreciated.
(Courtesy Irving House Historic Centre)

RICHMOND

LONDON FARM
Ca. 1885

Driving along the dyke toward London Farm emerging in the distance, one almost expects to see ladies in long turn-of-the-century voile dresses sipping tea on the farmhouse verandah. It is a quiet, contemplative place, set well back from the south arm of the Fraser River behind a screen of trees.

The farmhouse was built by George E. London, the original town planner of nearby Steveston. It was not only the center of London's 200-acre farm but served as a community center; church services were sometimes held in the living room. Part and parcel of the farm were a general store, a post office, and a landing area for boats plying the Fraser between Victoria and New Westminster. Restoration of the farmhouse, which began several years ago, is still under way. It is being refurnished in the style prevailing when London and his large family occupied the house.

Plans call for a Heritage Village where visitors may gain a sense of the period as they watch craftsmen duplicate works of the pioneer days. At present the farmhouse is open for tours, and picnicking facilities are provided on the lawn.

LONDON FARM, 6511 Dyke Road, Richmond, BC V6X 2P3; (604) 271-3922 or 271-3028. Located between Gilbert Road and No. 2 Road, east of Steveston.
Hours: July 1–September 4, 10–6 daily; September 5–July, 1–4 Monday–Friday.
Admission fee.
(Courtesy Richmond Historical and Museum Society)

SOOKE (NEAR VICTORIA)

MOSS COTTAGE
1870

When Mary Ellen Flynn set sail from Liverpool in 1869 to become the bride of James Welsh, she knew she would never see her old home and family again. Her husband-to-be was employed by the Muirs at Sooke, in the far-off colony of Vancouver Island, on Canada's west coast.

Soon after the Welshes' July wedding, the building of their new home was underway, with lumber cut by the Muirs' early steam sawmill. Mary Ellen called her new home "Moss Cottage" from her mother's family name, and it became a busy home for the Welshes and their family of young children. Over the years, this four-room cottage saw many families as occupants, but was always retained in the hands of the Welsh and Muir families, until 1977, when it was given to the Sooke Region Historical Society.

The Society moved the building two miles, to the site of the Sooke Region Museum, restored it, and furnished it with local pre-1900 furnishings. Built of vertical planking in "tidewater" style, it is the only remaining house of its type on Vancouver Island. Among the furnishings of interest are two hand-carved maple chairs which accompanied John Muir when he sailed around the Horn on the *Harpooner,* on his way to Vancouver Island to supervise the mining of coal for the Hudson's Bay Company.

The cottage furnishings show the day-to-day life of the early settlers and their families. As tours are escorted through, visitors hear the organ in the parlor (on tape), played by a Muir family descendant.

MOSS COTTAGE, P.O. Box 774/2070 Phillips Road, Sooke, BC V0S 1N0; (604) 642-3121. Located at corner of Sooke Road, 20 miles west of Victoria on Highway 14.
Hours: Summer, 10–6 daily; winter, 10–5 daily.
Admission by donation.
(Courtesy Sooke Region Historical Society)

VERNON

O'KEEFE HISTORIC RANCH 1892

This living museum of Okanagan Valley pioneer days is located on the fifteen-thousand-acre ranch established by Cornelius O'Keefe and his partners Thomas Wood and Thomas Greenhow in 1867. Nearly a century later, O'Keefe's youngest son Tierney and his wife re-created a pioneer settlement with authentic old buildings from the area. They are shown with period furnishings and artifacts.

The heart of the complex is the *O'Keefe House,* built by Cornelius in 1892 and occupied by the family until the 1970s. It is maintained as though the O'Keefes were out for the day, displaying many original furnishings and family possessions, among them a christening robe used by three generations of O'Keefe babies. Upstairs is a small room where the children learned their ABCs from a resident governess until they were old enough to be sent to boarding school.

Among the ranch outbuildings are a general store, a blacksmith shop, a collection of pioneer farm machinery, and St. Anne's Church, built in 1886 with donations from pioneer settlers of all faiths. Cornelius O'Keefe and Thomas Greenhow are buried in the old cemetery in unmarked graves.

O'KEEFE HISTORIC RANCH, P.O. Box 955/Highway 97, Vernon, BC V1T 6M8; (604) 542-7868. Located 7½ miles north of Vernon.
Hours: May 15–September 15, 9–5 daily. After September 15, available for tours by appointment.
Admission fee.
(Courtesy The O'Keefe Ranch and Interior Heritage Society)

VICTORIA

EMILY CARR HOUSE
1863

In reminiscences of her childhood in Victoria (*The Book of Small*), the great Canadian painter Emily Carr recalled her birthplace as a big, fine house by 1863 standards, on ten acres of fine land adjoining Beacon Hill Park. "It was all made of California redwood. The chimneys were of California brick and the mantelpieces of black marble. Every material used in the building of father's house was the very best, because he never bought anything cheap or shoddy."* "Father" was Richard Carr, an Englishman from Kent who arrived in British Columbia in 1863 with a modest fortune gained in California, along with his wife and Emily's two elder sisters. Within the year he had moved into this attractive Italianate villa designed by the Victoria architects Wright and Saunders. "Father wanted his place to look exactly like England," Emily remembered. "He planted cowslips and primroses and hawthorn hedges and all the Englishy flowers. He had stiles and meadows and took away all the wild Canadian'ness and made it as meek and English as he could."*

The spacious grounds of formal gardens, fruit orchards, cow paddocks, and the pond where Emily fished for tadpoles with an iron dipper are built over now, but the house itself has recently been restored to its original appearance. A visit to the Emily Carr Gallery at 1107 Wharf Street, where a film on her life is shown, is an informative complement to a tour of her home. Call 387-3080 for the film schedule.

EMILY CARR HOUSE, 207 Government Street, Victoria, BC V8V 2K8; (604) 387-6080.
Call for hours.
(Courtesy Province of British Columbia, Heritage Conservation Branch)

* Emily Carr, *The Book of Small* (Agincourt, Ontario: Clarke Irwin (1983), 1942).

207

VICTORIA

CRAIGDARROCH CASTLE 1888–90

Craigdarroch Castle fulfills a vow made by Robert Dunsmuir to his bride. As the story goes, Joan Olive White was reluctant to leave their native Scotland for the rigors and uncertainties of the Canadian wilderness. So Robert promised—if she would accompany him—a fairy tale future complete with liveried coachmen, diamond tiaras, and a castle with stained-glass windows and crystal chandeliers. The Ayreshire coalmaster's son did not confine himself to the Canadian wilderness, but carried coal with a fleet of ships from British Columbia to California (the California town of Dunsmuir was named in his honor), built up a conglomerate that included the Esquimault & Nanaimo Railroad, and founded a dynasty that has played a leading role in the life of British Columbia. He became a coal millionaire.

Robert did not live to see the completion of his promised castle, which he had named Craigdarroch for Annie Laurie's home in Dumfriesshire. Sited on a goodly elevation with a commanding view, the house was designed with elements of the Scottish Baronial, French Château, Jacobean, and Elizabethan styles under the aegis of Williams and Smith of Portland, Oregon. It is constructed of British Columbian granite. The majestic staircase rising from the baronial entry hall to the tower is thought to have been prefabricated in Chicago. The stained-glass windows probably came from Philadelphia. The scale of the castle is such that a modern three-bedroom house could be contained by the top-floor dancing hall. In its heyday it was surrounded by twenty-seven acres of formal gardens, oak groves, and orchards.

Sold by the Dunsmuirs after Joan Olive's death in 1908, Craigdarroch is being meticulously restored. Period antiques and paintings evoke the Dunsmuir era.

CRAIGDARROCH CASTLE, 1050 Joan Crescent, Victoria, BC V8S 3L5; (604) 592-5323.
Hours: Open daily. Winter, 10–5:30; summer, 9–9:30.
Admission by donation.
(Courtesy Society for the Maintenance and Preservation of Craigdarroch Castle)

VICTORIA

CRAIGFLOWER MANOR
1853–56

One of Vancouver Island's most appealing historic homes is Craigflower, manor house of one of the last of four farms established by the Hudson's Bay Company to substantiate the terms of its lease of the island. This two-story Georgian-style wooden house, built by the farm's bailiff Kenneth McKenzie to resemble his family home in Scotland, was constructed almost entirely of materials produced on the farm. The massive oak front door reinforced with iron studs, and the heavy wooden shutters that can be closed from the inside, were once thought to afford protection against Indian attack, but are now given a less colorful interpretation. The decorative ironwork (fashioned by the farm's blacksmith Peter Bartelman) was considered the hallmark of a gentleman; the wooden shutters served as insulation against summer heat and cold. Unusual features are the arbutus-veneer handrail of the staircase, *chef d'oeuvre* of a Company carpenter, Henry Wain, and the Gothic arch motif used in the front door fanlight and the bedroom fireplaces.

Craigflower Manor now stands on a fraction of its original acreage, shorn of its bakery (which supplied all Victoria with baked goods), sawmill, kiln, smithy, and outbuildings, but restored and furnished most attractively to portray life during the McKenzies' occupancy. Some of their possessions are among the items displayed. The manor also had its own schoolhouse, which still stands beside Gorge Inlet, just across the bridge. Built between 1854 and 1855, it is the oldest schoolhouse still standing in Western Canada.

CRAIGFLOWER MANOR, 110 Island Highway, Victoria, BC V9B 1E9; (604) 387-3067.
Hours: May 16–September 15, 10–5 Tuesday–Sunday; September 16–May 15, 10–4 Wednesday–Sunday.
(Courtesy Province of British Columbia, Heritage Conservation Branch)

VICTORIA

HELMCKEN HOUSE
1852

British Columbia's oldest residence is a rambling, picturesque structure in the English rural style, clearly showing its evolution from the single-story log cabin built for the Hudson's Bay Company physician John Sebastian Helmcken and his bride. In his memoirs Helmcken left a vivid portrait of the difficulties of building even this simple structure. As there were no contractors "everything had to be done piecemeal . . . There being no lumber, it had to be built with logs squared at two sides and 6" thick . . . Well, the timber had to be taken from the forest—squared there and brought down by water. All this had to be contracted for by French Canadians, then when brought to the beach—I had [to] beg oxen of the Company to haul it to the site. Then other Canadians took the job of putting the building up as far as the logs were concerned—and then shingling—the Indian at this time made shingles—all split."*

All the hardware for the house came around the Horn from Britain. Anxious to be finished by the spring, the doctor found the expense and annoyances very great, possibly because while all this was going on, "I was 'courting'."*

Purchased by the government of British Columbia on the death of Dr. Helmcken's youngest daughter in 1939, Helmcken House is essentially unchanged and contains furnishings and mementoes accumulated by the Helmckens over more than seventy years. Other pioneer items supplement their possessions.

HELMCKEN HOUSE, 638 Elliot Street, Victoria, BC V8V 1W1; (604) 387-3440. Located adjacent to the Provincial Museum.
Hours: May 16–September 15, 10–4 daily; September 16–May 15, 10–4 Tuesday–Sunday.
(Courtesy Province of British Columbia, Heritage Conservation Branch)

* Dorothy Blakey Smith, ed., *The Reminiscences of Doctor John Sebastian Helmcken* (Vancouver: University of British Columbia Press, 1975).

VICTORIA

POINT ELLICE HOUSE
Ca. 1863

Sheltered from Rock Bay's industries by a screen of trees and old-fashioned gardens, this picturesque residence in the Italianate style was the home of Peter O'Reilly, one of British Columbia's first gold commissioners and county court judges. O'Reilly was of the Irish gentry and had served seven years with the Irish Revenue Police before emigrating to British Columbia in 1859. He seems to have carried out his duties with flair: confronting unruly miners in the Kootenays, he is said to have quelled them with a calm "Now, boys, there must be no shooting, for if there is shooting, there will surely be a hanging." In 1863 O'Reilly married Caroline Agnes Trutch, the sister of Joseph Trutch, British Columbia's first lieutenant-governor.

Little is known about Point Ellice House before the O'Reillys bought it in 1868. Between 1863 and 1889 there were substantial alterations. The house now preserves an unusually rich collection of Victorian antiques, period clothing, furnishings, and memorabilia accumulated by three generations of the O'Reilly family. No other house open to the public in Victoria affords as intimate a portrait of life from the 1860s to the present.

POINT ELLICE HOUSE, 2616 Pleasant Street, Victoria, BC V8T 4V3; (604) 385-3837.
Hours: May 16–September 15, 10–5, Tuesday–Sunday; September 16–May 15, 12–4, Tuesday–Sunday.
(Courtesy Province of British Columbia, Heritage Conservation Branch)

VICTORIA

REGENTS PARK HOUSE
1885

This striking Italianate villa was built on a ten-acre estate by D. W. Higgins, editor and publisher of *The British Colonist* during the last decades of the nineteenth century, and speaker of the British Columbia Provincial Legislature between 1886 and 1895. There is a particularly impressive grand staircase here, eight High Victorian fireplaces, and elaborate plasterwork. Regents Park House now displays an extensive collection of Victoriana assembled over a period of thirty years by present owner Carl Rudolph. His sympathetic restoration of the house earned Heritage Canada's 1975 Award of Honour.

REGENTS PARK HOUSE, 1501 Fort Street, Victoria, BC V8S 3L5.
Hours: May–October, 1–6 daily.
Admission fee.
(Courtesy Carl Rudolph)

IDAHO

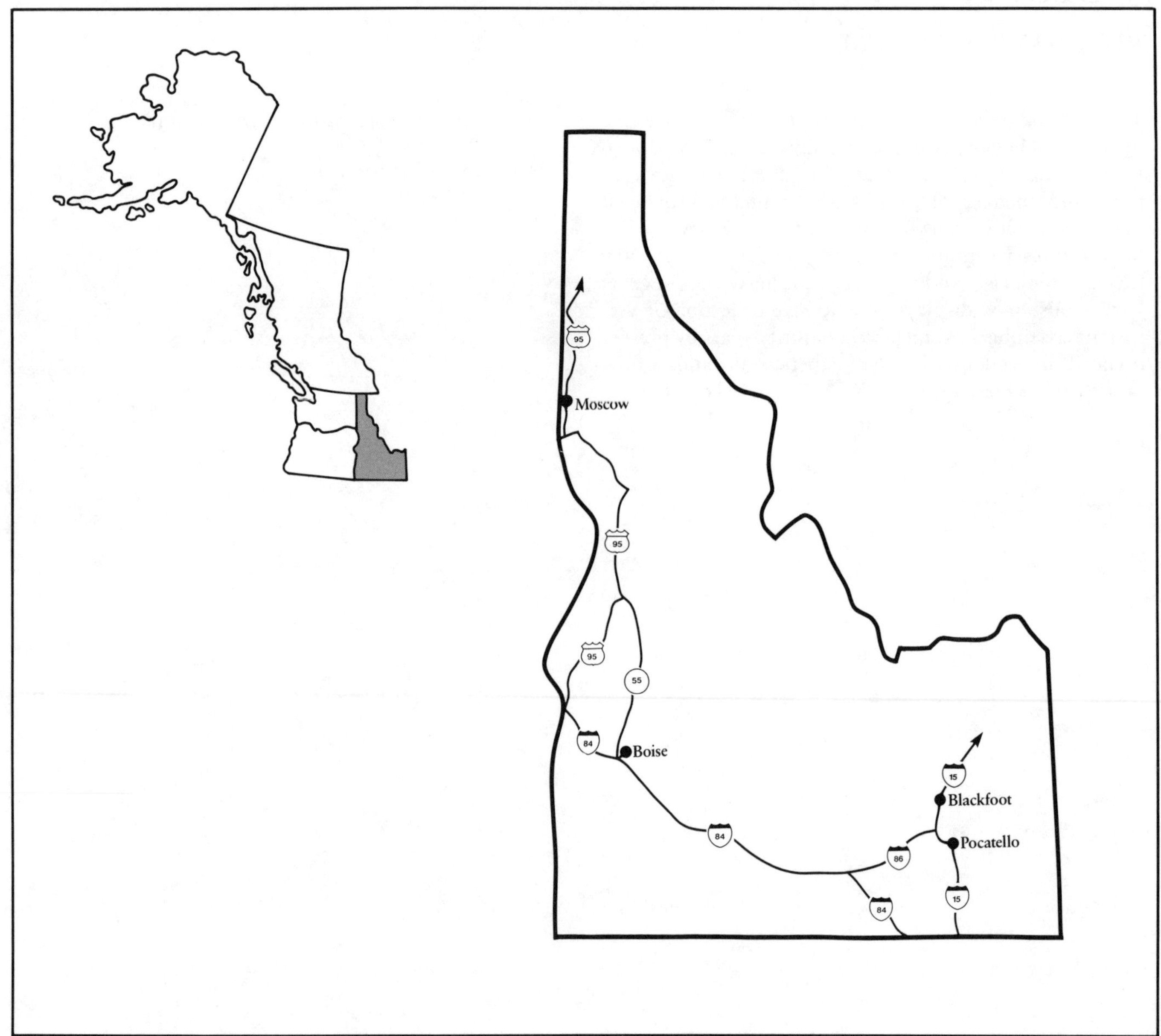

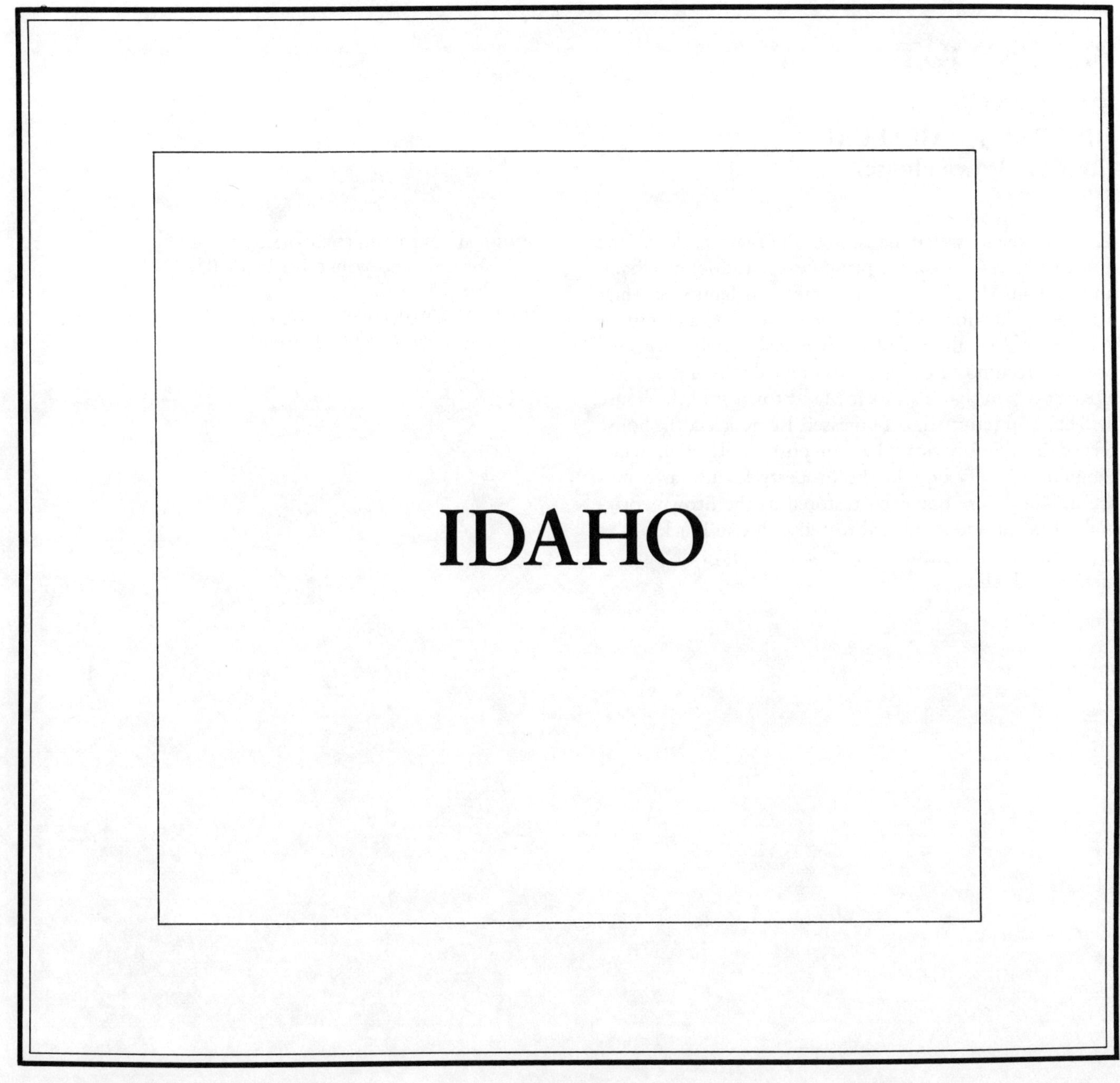

IDAHO

BLACKFOOT

BINGHAM COUNTY HISTORICAL MUSEUM (John G. Brown House) 1905

This eclectically styled mansion built of lava rock was the home of John G. Brown, a prominent Blackfoot merchant, and his wife May. The Browns were from Tennessee. Their arrival in Blackfoot with a Chinese cook and a chauffeur and the parties they held in their elaborately furnished home were almost instantly part of local folklore.

After her husband's death May Brown sold the house in 1927 and returned to Tennessee. Remodeled, the house served as an American Legion post until 1974, when Bingham County bought the property for use as a museum. The house has been restored as the Browns originally built it and furnished to reflect life in Blackfoot at the turn of the century. There are displays of pioneer history and relics.

BINGHAM COUNTY HISTORICAL MUSEUM, 190 North Shilling Avenue, Blackfoot, ID 83221; (208) 785-5005.

Hours: 1–5 Wednesday–Friday.

(Courtesy Bingham County Historical Society)

MUSEUM
BINGHAM COUNTY HISTORICAL
MUSEUM

BOISE

THE BISHOPS' HOUSE
Ca. 1880; enlarged 1899

The former residence of Boise's Episcopal bishops was originally a simple frame dwelling built in the 1880s to serve as the rectory. When the Rt. Rev. James Bowen Funsten was elected to the bishopric in 1899, the rectory was remodeled to provide a gracious home for him, his wife, and their five daughters. For three thousand dollars, Tourtellotte & Company, architects of the Idaho Statehouse, added four rooms, a tower, and wide porches in the Queen Anne style.

Threatened with demolition in 1974, the house was moved from its original site at Second and Idaho streets to its present location and restored; it now serves the community as a center for a variety of social activities. Although the Bishops' House is not a museum, appointments may be made to visit it. The main floor has been refurbished in the style of 1899, the year of Bishop Funsten's remodeling, and retains its original hardwood floors, woodwork, and glass.

THE BISHOPS' HOUSE, 2420 Old Penitentiary Road, Boise, ID 83702.
Admission by appointment. Contact the Bishops' House coordinator, (208) 342-3279.
(Courtesy Friends of the Bishops' House, Inc.)

BOISE

JOHN O'FARRELL CABIN
1863

John O'Farrell, a native of County Tyrone, Ireland, built this log cabin in the summer of 1863. Preserved unfurnished, there is little to see through its single unshuttered window, but it has the distinction of being one of the first buildings erected in Boise. Because O'Farrell's wife recognized two travel-stained men riding by the cabin as priests and insisted that he ride after them, the cabin came to serve Boise's Roman Catholics as a place of worship for several years.

O'Farrell began his adventurous career in 1838 at the age of fifteen, aboard a vessel of the Orient Steamship Line plying between London and Calcutta. He joined the U.S. Navy before the Mexican War of 1846, knew California while it was still a Mexican province, fought for Queen Victoria in the Crimean War, and made the first discovery of gold in the Pike's Peak country of Colorado before settling in Boise in 1863.

JOHN O'FARRELL CABIN, Fort Street (near Fifth), Boise, ID 83702. May be viewed from exterior only.
(Courtesy Idaho State Historical Society)

BOISE

PIONEER VILLAGE

The Idaho State Historical Society has relocated four of Boise's early cabins and houses to a site adjacent to the Society's museum in Julia Davis Park. Two, the Isaac N. Coston and I. B. Pierce cabins, are traditionally believed to be the first dwellings erected in Boise (for a third, see the John O'Farrell Cabin). These buildings may be viewed from the exterior at any time. You must make an appointment in advance to visit Mayor Thomas E. Logan's house.

Isaac N. Coston Cabin

1863

Formerly located east of Boise, this cabin was built by a New York lawyer who came to Idaho in 1862; after two years of mining he settled as a farmer in the Boise Valley. Coston represented Ada County in the state legislatures of 1870, 1872, and 1876.

I. B. Pierce Cabin

1863

When Mary Pierce, widow of the Boise pioneer I. B. Pierce, visited Boise in 1903, she identified this small cabin as one she and her husband had occupied in 1863. Bound for Oregon, they had crossed the plains behind ox teams, but when they reached the Boise Valley they found it too lovely to pass by. A blacksmith, Pierce found employment at Fort Boise (then a tent city). On Sundays, according to Mrs. Pierce, he took his oxen and hauled logs from the river to build the cabin. About a year later he built a larger home and used the cabin as his blacksmith shop. The cabin is known to have served later as a jail and as the home of a Chinese family at the turn of the century.

Mayor Thomas E. Logan House

1865

This attractive single-story adobe home with a porch is the sole survivor of the many adobe buildings erected in Boise during the 1860s. The house, built by Thomas E. Logan, four times mayor of Boise and postmaster during the 1870s, was constructed of adobe bricks made on its original site on Sixth Street. Its barn-red coat of paint was applied soon after completion. The porch is a reconstruction of one shown in an early photograph of the house. Logan House is furnished with period antiques, and a portion of the wall has been stripped of several layers of wallpaper to reveal the adobe construction.

Richard C. Adelmann House

Ca. 1878

The Adelmann House is largely a reconstruction of the original wood-frame home of one of Boise's German pioneers. Richard Adelmann came to the United States as a child of eight and was only seventeen when he ran away from home to serve in the Union Army during the Civil War. In 1872 he came to Boise where, after working at several jobs, he became the owner of the Gem Saloon and a part-owner of the Sorrel Horse mine, for a time one of the richest gold mines in Idaho.

PIONEER VILLAGE, Julia Davis Park, Boise, ID 83702; for information, call Idaho State Historical Society, (208) 334-2120.
Museum hours: 9–5 daily.
(Courtesy Idaho State Historical Society)

MOSCOW

McCONNELL MANSION
1886

William E. McConnell, twice governor of Idaho and the state's second U.S. senator, began building this imposing two-story clapboard mansion in the Eastlake style in July 1886. By late December, for an expenditure of $60,000, the house was ready for occupation.

McConnell came to Moscow in 1878 after farming and operating a string of pack horses in southern Idaho. In Moscow he turned to merchandising, opening a general store at what is now First and Main streets. The venture prospered, and by 1891 McConnell and his partners were able to build one of the largest stores in the Pacific Northwest. He was elected governor in 1892. Though he was successful politically, his business ventures were another matter. During the 1893 depression he and his partners went bankrupt. To save the McConnell home, Mrs. McConnell declared a homestead on the mansion; eventually they were forced to sell it to Dr. William Adair in 1901.

Bequeathed to Latah County by its last owner, Dr. Frederic C. Church, the McConnell Mansion is now a museum of local history. Although altered over the years, the mansion is regarded as a good example of early Idaho architecture, and it has been furnished with Victorian antiques. The governor's official portrait hangs in the former parlor.

MCCONNELL MANSION, 110 South Adams,
Moscow, ID 83843; (208) 882-1004.
Hours: 1–4 Wednesday–Sunday.
(Courtesy Latah County Historical Society)

SECOND ST. 400 E

POCATELLO

STANDROD HOUSE
1895–1902

The home of Judge Drew W. Standrod was one of the most impressive residences built in Idaho in its day. Standrod built himself a twelve-room, castlelike structure of handcut local sandstone with Norman and Byzantine turrets, multiple chimneys, spacious porches, and a steeply pitched roof characteristic of the Renaissance. The rich ornamentation and palatial scale of the house reflected Standrod's position in the community. He began his career as district attorney in 1886 and went on to serve as district judge and as a member of Idaho's constitutional convention.

After Judge Standrod's death in the 1940s, the house suffered greatly from neglect until the city of Pocatello purchased and restored it as their bicentennial project. Now used as a cultural center, it is furnished with antiques of the period 1890–1910; only the pump organ belonged to the Standrods. A notable feature is the woodwork: all original, it includes parquet flooring imported from France and finely wrought scrollwork. Some of the original cut glass light shades remain.

STANDROD HOUSE, 648 North Garfield Road,
Pocatello, ID 83201; (208) 232-9570.
Hours: 10–1 Tuesday–Friday.
(Courtesy Standrod Preservation Society)

OREGON

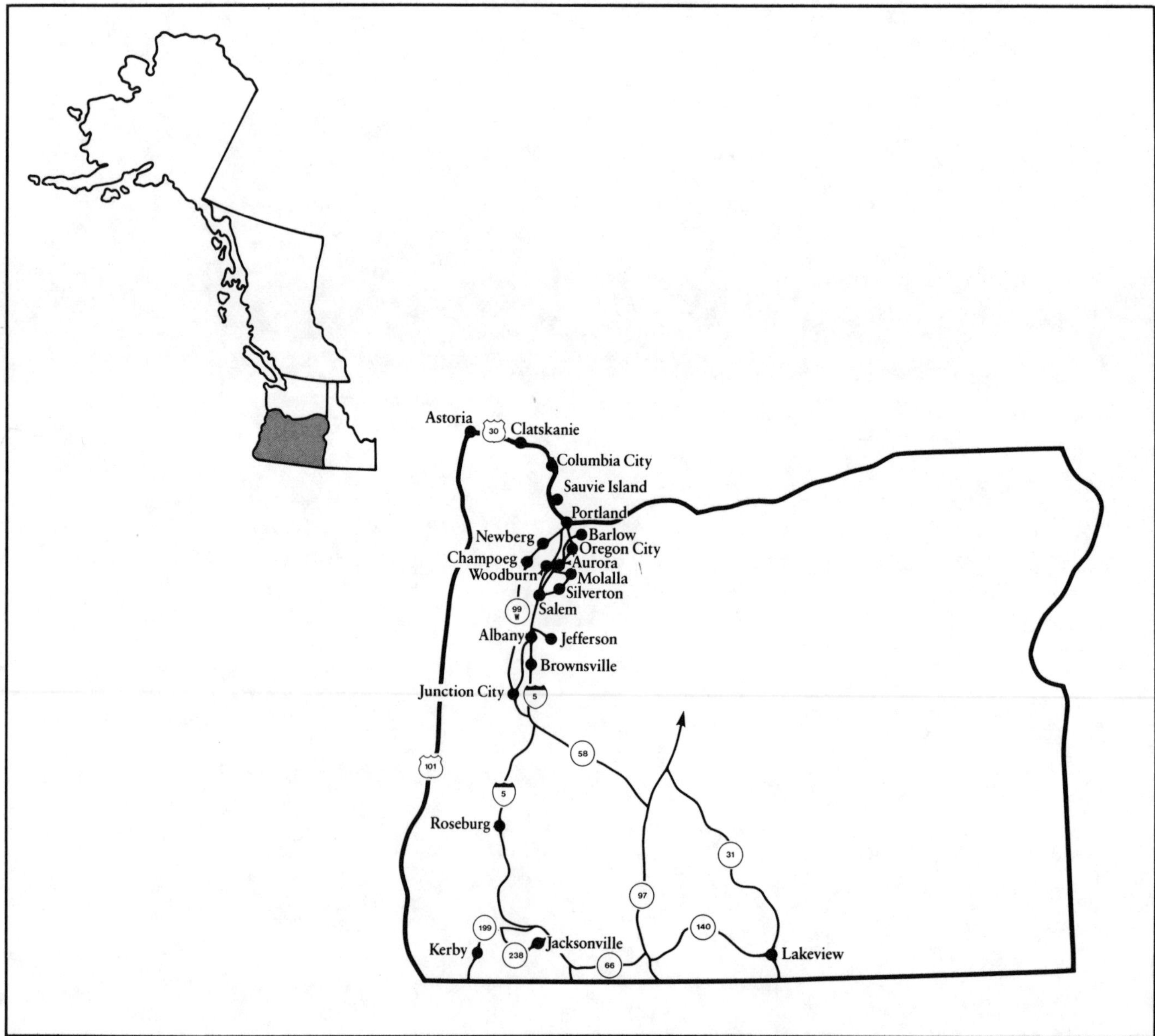

Astoria
30
Clatskanie
Columbia City
Sauvie Island
Portland
Newberg
Barlow
Champoeg
Oregon City
Aurora
Woodburn
Molalla
Silverton
99 W
Salem
Albany
Jefferson
Brownsville
Junction City
5
58
101
5
Roseburg
31
97
199
140
Jacksonville
Kerby
238
66
Lakeview

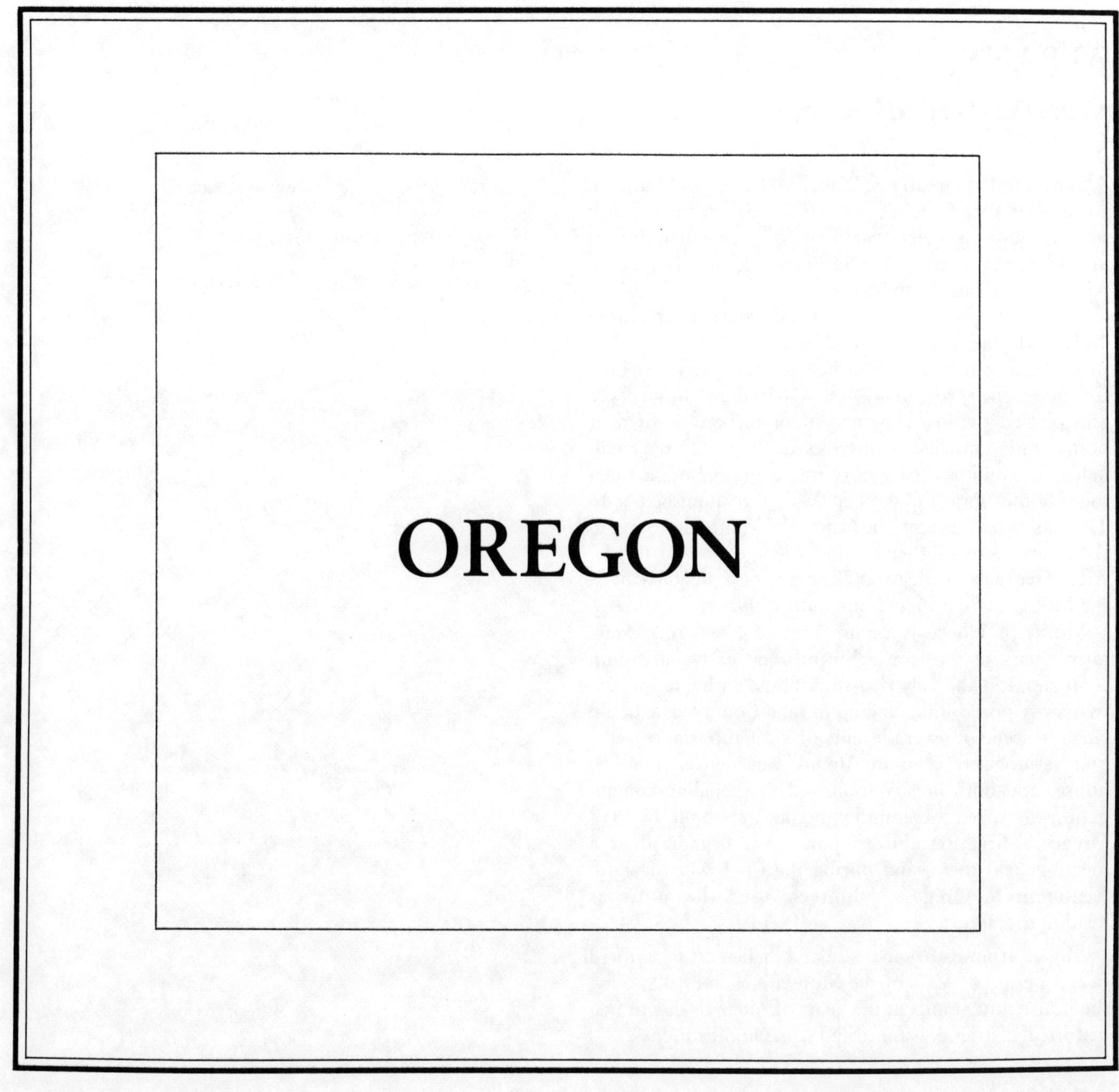

OREGON

ALBANY

MONTEITH HOUSE
Ca. 1849

Albany's founding fathers, Walter and Thomas Monteith, were New York State Yankees of Scottish descent, which may account for their bargaining skills. They paid Hiram Smead "a cayuse pony and $100 in cash" for the land on which Albany now stands.

These enterprising young men had crossed the plains in 1847 and signed up for a spell in the Cayuse Indian War in southeastern Washington before they arrived in Linn County in the spring of 1848. By 1850 they had surveyed and platted the town, named it for the capital of their home state, enriched themselves in the California goldfields, and built this two-story frame house. Both made it their home until 1855 when Walter relinquished it to Thomas and his bride. The last of the Monteiths to live in the house were another brother, George, and his family. After George's death in 1877, his widow operated it as the Monteith Boarding House until 1900.

Monteith House is reminiscent of New York State farmhouses of the late eighteenth and early nineteenth centuries. It is the only two-story house with a full-length two-story porch still standing in Linn County. The house was the scene of several events of local importance—the first sermon preached in Albany was delivered in the house, and both Presbyterian and Episcopalian congregations gathered there until churches were built. In 1857 Oregon's first Republican party was organized at a meeting held there, and during the Civil War the Fifth Regiment of Oregon Volunteers used the house as headquarters.

Moved from its original site and meticulously restored over a period of years by the Monteith Historical Society, the house now stands in the heart of Albany's downtown historical district. It is furnished with period antiques.

MONTEITH HOUSE, 518 Southwest Second Avenue, Albany, OR 97321; (503) 967-8699.
Hours: By appointment only.
Admission fee.
(Courtesy Monteith Historical Society)

ASTORIA

CLATSOP COUNTY HISTORICAL MUSEUM (Old Flavel Mansion) 1883–87

This elegant example of modified Queen Anne–style architecture was designed by a San Francisco architect for Capt. George Flavel, one of the Pacific Coast's ablest seamen and entrepreneurs. He was also a hero, presented a gold medal by the people of Portland for his heroism in rescuing survivors of the *General Warren,* wrecked on the Columbia River bar in 1852. The house retains many evidences of Captain Flavel's luxurious tastes—notable are the hand-carved rosewood, mahogany, walnut, and maple fireplaces, the highly polished paneling of rare woods, and the imported European tiles. Occupied by his descendants until 1933, the house is now the Clatsop County Historical Museum.

CLATSOP COUNTY HISTORICAL MUSEUM (Old Flavel Mansion), 441 Eighth Street, Astoria, OR 97103; (503) 325-2203.
Hours: May 1–October 1, 10–5 daily; October 2–April 30, 12–5 Tuesday–Sunday.
Admission fee.
(Courtesy Clatsop County Historical Society)

AURORA

OX BARN MUSEUM COMPLEX

Between 1856 and 1877, Aurora was the setting of an experiment in Christian communal living under the leadership of a Dr. William Keil. Moved as much by the prospect of an environment undisturbed by influences that could weaken his authority as by the Oregon Territory's fertile lands, Dr. Keil led a band of some six hundred German idealists from their settlement in Bethel, Missouri, to the new promised land. The colony they established at Aurora was by all accounts a most pleasant place to live, renowned for good cooking, good music, and the excellence of its household crafts. But it did not long survive Keil's death in 1877. Today about thirty buildings dating from the colony era survive; four, known as the Ox Barn Museum Complex, are open to the public.

Kraus House

1862–64

This two-story frame house with hip roof was moved to the museum complex from its original colony site. Built mainly of rough, oversized pieces of unfinished lumber, it follows the typical colony plan of two rooms on each floor, which lead off a stairway, a storage attic, and a pantry underneath the stair. Porches front and rear enliven the plain facade. Donated by descendants of its original owners Elizabeth Giesy and her husband George Kraus, the house is furnished much as it was during their occupancy, with furniture handmade by the colonists.

Steinbach Cabin

1876

This sturdy three-room cabin, built by George and Catherine Steinbach on a site five miles north of Aurora, is considered a good example of the colonists' building skills. Constructed of peeled and hand-hewn timbers chinked with mud, manure, and straw, the cabin also demonstrates pioneer thrift and ingenuity—newspapers covered the interior walls for insulation, and a fireplace was built out into the room, so that no heat was lost through a back wall. The furnishings, though not original to the cabin, are authentic antiques of the colony.

Ox Barn Museum

1859–60

In its time an ox barn, a horse barn, a stage depot, a store, and a home, this building now houses colony furniture and artifacts. The washhouse on the grounds, where women worked together at such chores as canning fruit, boiling clothes, and making soap, suggests the colony lifestyle.

OX BARN MUSEUM COMPLEX, P.O. Box 202/
Second and Liberty streets (one block from Highway 99E), Aurora, OR 97002; (503) 678-5754.

Hours: 1–5, Tuesday–Sunday during June, July, August; 1–5, Wednesday–Sunday rest of year. Guided tours.

Admission fee.

(Courtesy Aurora Colony Historical Society)

BARLOW

WILLIAM BARLOW HOUSE 1885

This two-story Italianate mansion built by William Barlow in the late 1800s was, during his lifetime, the center of a large farm that had its own way station and warehouse on the Southern Pacific Railroad. Barlow, a well-known entrepreneur in Oregon's early days who was among the originators of the Oregon State Fair, early saw that Oregon was well suited to fruit farming. His apple nursery was the second to be established in the state. In 1852 he began to experiment with black walnuts, importing a bushel of nuts by way of the Horn. He planted the splendid avenue of black walnut trees that leads from the highway to his home.

Barlow House, still a private home today, is shown with many of its original furnishings.

WILLIAM BARLOW HOUSE, 24670 South Highway 99E, Barlow (near Canby), OR 97013; (503) 266-4375.

Hours: 1–5 Sunday. Closed January and February. Guided tours only.

Admission fee.

(Courtesy Virginia L. Miller)

BROWNSVILLE

MOYER HOUSE HISTORIC HOME 1878–81

Brownsville's first mayor, John M. Moyer, began building this Italian villa–style home for himself and his wife Elizabeth in 1878. From its third-story cupola Moyer could look down on a business "empire" that included the Bank of Brownsville, woollen mills, and the lumber mill that provided the choice woods used in his residence. residence.

Moyer's early efforts to make his fortune had not been successful. He arrived at Linn County in 1852 and, being a carpenter by trade, was soon at work. After finishing the home of Brownsville's founding father, J. M. Brown, he sought quick profit by driving cattle to California; he returned to Brownsville almost penniless. In 1862 he tried again, this time in the Idaho gold mines; he lost eight hundred dollars before returning to Brownsville. With the purchase of Brownsville's planing mill in 1863 his luck changed, and by 1878 Moyer could celebrate his success by building a home regarded as "truly beautiful and commodious."

Moyer House is shown today with period furnishings, among them the Moyers' stately mantel clock, and parlor chairs crafted by Linn County's first cabinetmaker, Charles Mealey. Restoration has revealed oil-painted stencil designs on the ceilings of the main floor and twin circular staircases leading to the second story.

MOYER HOUSE HISTORIC HOME, 204 Main Street, Brownsville, OR 97327; (503) 466-3070.
Hours: June–October, 11–4 Tuesday–Sunday; October–May, 11–4 Saturday and Sunday.
Admission by donation.
(Courtesy Linn County Museum)

CHAMPOEG

ROBERT NEWELL HOUSE
1852

On a hillside overlooking the Willamette River stands the home of Robert Newell, the mountain man from Zanesville, Ohio, who in 1840 brought the first wagons from Fort Hall into the Willamette Valley by way of the Columbia River.

Newell played a significant role in Oregon's early history as a member of the committee that framed the territory's first laws, and he was twice speaker of the house. Whatever position he held, throughout his life he had a reputation for integrity. He settled in Champoeg about 1842 and by the 1850s had established a gristmill there as well as a riverboat operation between Oregon City and Willamette Falls. His home was a little above the highest point of the December flood of 1861; so generous was he in helping his distressed neighbors that he ran into financial difficulties as a result. His Champoeg farmhouse, completely restored, now serves as a museum of local history.

ROBERT NEWELL HOUSE, 8089 Champoeg Road N.E., Champoeg, near St. Paul, OR 97137 (west of Champoeg State Park); (503) 678-5537.

Hours: 12–5 Tuesday–Sunday. Closed December and January.

Admission fee.

(Courtesy Oregon State Society of the Daughters of the American Revolution)

CHAMPOEG

PIONEER MOTHER'S MEMORIAL CABIN 1931

Located in Champoeg State Park, this replica of a pioneer log cabin stands but a few yard's from the site where, on May 2, 1843, Oregon Territory settlers voted to establish the provisional government that paved the way for Oregon's admission to the Union. Dedicated to the memory of the pioneer mothers of the Willamette River Valley, the cabin is furnished with items belonging to the state's early families.

PIONEER MOTHER'S MEMORIAL CABIN, Champoeg Park, 8035 Champoeg Road N.E., Champoeg, near St. Paul, OR 97137; (503) 633-2237.

Hours: 12–5 Tuesday–Sunday. Closed December and January.

Admission fee.

(Courtesy Oregon State Society of the Daughters of the American Revolution)

CLATSKANIE

THOMAS J. FLIPPIN HOUSE
1898–1900

"A man's home is his castle, and so I built mine to look like one," said Thomas J. Flippin of the splendid mansion he built high on a hill above Clatskanie. Flippin had a right to his pride for he had successfully lived the American dream. By the time he was thirty he had worked his way up from a lowly "gypo" logger to owner of a sawmill on Roaring Creek.

Flippin House was built by Markwell & Sons of San Andreas, California. With its two round towers, steep gabled roof, fish scale tiles, and classical porch the house suggests, if it does not replicate, a French Renaissance château. Its restoration and furnishings bring it as close as possible to its original state at the turn of the century.

THOMAS J. FLIPPIN HOUSE, 620 Tichnor Street, Clatskanie, OR 97016; (503) 728-3608 or 728-2026.
Hours: 11–4 daily.
Admission fee.
(Courtesy Clatskanie Senior Citizens)

COLUMBIA CITY

CAPLES HOUSE
1870

Set apart by a low white picket fence, Caples House conveys a rather prim first impression, which belies the warmth of its interior. The two-story house was built by Dr. Charles Green Caples, who came to Oregon Territory by wagon train in 1844 as a boy of twelve. It's a good example of an American pioneer family home, complete with most of its original furnishings. The adjoining carriage house now contains period clothing and an outstanding display of antique dolls and toys.

Caples seems to have been of true pioneer stuff. Within a few years of arriving in Oregon he was off to the California goldfields to seek his fortune. On returning, he enrolled at Tualatin Academy (now Pacific University) and went on to apprentice himself as a physician. He also turned his hand proficiently to cabinetry—a number of pieces of furniture in the house were made by him.

CAPLES HOUSE, 1915 First Street, Columbia City, OR 97018; (503) 397-5390.
Hours: February–November, 11–5 Wednesday–Saturday; 1–6 Sunday.
Admission fee.
(Courtesy Oregon State Society of the Daughters of the American Revolution)

JACKSONVILLE

BEEKMAN HOUSE
1876

Time seems scarcely to have touched this two-story Victorian Gothic house built by Cornelius C. Beekman, an early Wells Fargo agent and Jacksonville's first banker. Surrounded by an old-fashioned garden and furnished with Beekman family possessions, it now presents, as though preserved in amber, an intimate portrait of late-Victorian life in a small Western city.

Cornelius Beekman's progress from apprentice carpenter to founder of the second bank in the Pacific Northwest is a classic pioneer tale. He was born in New York of a Dutch family first established in New Amsterdam in the 1630s. He was only twenty-two when in 1850 he set out for the California fields. Combining carpentry and gold mining at Scott's Bar, he rapidly accumulated a small working capital. By 1855 he had established a pony express service between Yreka and Jacksonville that became a legend: riding alone at night across the Siskiyou Mountains, he packed millions of dollars in gold dust and coin and never lost a dollar. At the same time he operated an office in Jacksonville for the purchase of gold dust. For the convenience of his customers, he began to accept deposits. Old-timers liked to recall Beekman's ways. No receipts were given for deposits; withdrawals were made without checks (indeed he asked anyone wanting a checking system to take his business elsewhere). Yet no accounting was ever asked of Beekman, and his bank rode serenely through the financial panics of 1873, 1893, and 1907, able to secure other banks with large loans. In 1912, at the age of eighty-four, he announced his retirement. His depositors refused to take their money elsewhere, so Cornelius Beekman stayed in business until his death in 1915.

BEEKMAN HOUSE, 325 East California Street, Jacksonville, OR 97530. For information, call the Southern Oregon Historical Society, (503) 899-1847.
Hours: Memorial Day–Labor Day, 1–5 daily. Closed during winter.
(Courtesy Southern Oregon Historical Society)

JACKSONVILLE

CATHOLIC RECTORY
1860s; enlarged 1891

Originally a private home, this Gothic clapboard cottage served as the rectory of St. Joseph's Catholic Church from 1875 until 1908. A small rear addition was built about 1891, and the front porch supposedly was added at the same time. The interior is furnished in the style of the 1870s.

CATHOLIC RECTORY, 202 North Fourth Street,
Jacksonville, OR 97530. For information,
call the Southern Oregon Historical Society;
(503) 899-1847.
Hours: Memorial Day–Labor Day, 1–5 daily.
Closed during winter.
Admission fee.

JACKSONVILLE

McCULLY HOUSE
1854–60

Jacksonville's first physician, Dr. John Wilmer McCully, and his wife Jane began this handsome Classical Revival home in 1854. Shortly after it was finished in 1860, Dr. McCully left Jacksonville for the mines of Montana and Idaho. His descendants lived on in the house until the 1940s (it is still a private residence). The richly furnished interior contains American antiques spanning three hundred years. Many pieces belonged to the McCully family. Of special interest is a doll collection, with a doll representative of every well-known doll manufacturer from 1640 to the present.

McCULLY HOUSE, 240 California Street,
Jacksonville, OR 97530; (503) 899-1942.
Open for viewing in the summer months only.
(Courtesy Edwin K. and Edna Meadows)

JACKSONVILLE

JEREMIAH NUNAN HOUSE
1892

Multigabled and sporting exuberant ornamentation, iron trimming, and a flamboyant brick chimney, the Jeremiah Nunan House is a fine example of the Queen Anne style popular in the last decades of the nineteenth century. Nunan had ordered his house up from Knoxville, Tennessee, in kit form (complete with a foreman to supervise assembly) from *The Cottage Souvenir,* a catalogue of house plans by George F. Barber. For $7,792, including freight, materials, and labor, Nunan acquired a three-story mansion with twenty-two rooms, including a twenty-four-hundred-square-foot ballroom on the third floor.

Jeremiah and Delia Nunan, both Irish immigrants, had come to Jacksonville in the 1860s. Starting in business as a saddle and tack maker (while Delia took in sewing), Nunan eventually opened a general merchandise store that prospered rapidly. Successful in his mining and ranching ventures as well, by the 1890s he was reckoned one of the wealthiest men in the area.

Today, the Jeremiah Nunan House is still a private home, meticulously restored by its present owners to the early Nunan period. A feature of the interior worthy of special attention is the variety of woods used in the doors, paneling, and trim, particularly the rare bird's-eye pine. The original carriage house, well house, and wood shed still stand on the grounds.

JEREMIAH NUNAN HOUSE, 635 North Oregon Street, Jacksonville, OR 97530; (503) 899-1890.

Hours: May–September, 12–4 Monday–Saturday; October–April, 12–4 Saturday only. Guided tours. Groups may make advance reservations.

Admission fee.

(Courtesy Richard Lucier)

JEFFERSON

JACOB CONSER HOUSE
1854

This two-story Colonial-style house was the first frame building erected in Jefferson. Its builder, Jacob Conser, had two other notable firsts to his credit: he established the first ferry across the Santiam River here, and in 1853 he built the town's first sawmill. The Conser House has served as a pony express stop, a home, and a hotel among whose guests was Gen. Phillip Sheridan. Conser's large clock with wooden gears is preserved in the library.

JACOB CONSER HOUSE, 114 Main Street, Jefferson, OR 97352.
For admission, inquire at city offices, 163 Main Street, Monday–Friday, 8–5; (503) 327-2768.
(Courtesy City of Jefferson)

JUNCTION CITY

DR. NORMAN L. LEE HOUSE
Pre-1871; enlarged 1878

The home of Junction City's first physician, Dr. Norman L. Lee, combines a single-story structure moved from Lancaster in 1871 and the two-story portion built on the site by Dr. Lee in 1878. Considered a good example of the late nineteenth century Western farmhouse style, it is constructed entirely of wood fastened with square, hand-forged nails. Although remodeled over the years, the house still retains several original windows with handmade shutters. Dr. Lee's belief that light and air were fundamental to good health was expressed in the high ceilings and large windows that characterize his home.

As children the doctor and his wife, Amanda Griggs Lee, had crossed the plains in covered wagons with their parents. Lee's parents settled in Oregon in 1847, first in Portland, then in Salem, before taking up donation land in Lebanon. He acquired the rudiments of his medical profession while serving in the Oregon Infantry during the Civil War, and later went on to become one of the first graduates of Willamette University. He practiced medicine in Lancaster until the new railroad bypassed the town in favor of Junction City two miles away.

Lee House now serves as Junction City's history museum, displaying not only memorabilia of pioneer families but Indian artifacts as well.

DR. NORMAN L. LEE HOUSE, 655 Holly Street, Junction City, OR 97448; (503) 998-6154, 998-8554, 998-6714, or 998-8985.

Hours: Open 2–5 last Sunday of each month, during annual Scandinavian Festival, and by appointment.

(Courtesy Linn County Historical Society)

KERBY

STITH-NAUCKE HOUSE
(Kerbyville Museum)
1870s

The addition of a second-floor balcony in 1916 is the only change made to the exterior of this two-story wood-frame house since it was built for William Naucke by Frank Stith in the 1870s. Furnished with nineteenth-century antiques and artifacts from pioneer Illinois Valley homes, it is maintained by Josephine County as a museum of local history.

STITH-NAUCKE HOUSE, Kerbyville Museum, U.S. Highway 199, Kerby, OR 97531; (503) 592-2076.
Hours: May–October, 10–5 daily; November–April, by appointment.
(Courtesy Kerbyville Museum)

LAKEVIEW

SCHMINCK MEMORIAL MUSEUM 1922

This modest stucco bungalow houses the Lula and Dalpheus Schminck collection of more than four thousand artifacts relating to everyday life in Lake County during the nineteenth and early-twentieth centuries. The rather unusual collection is the result of the Schmincks' lifelong habit of saving things—Victorian furniture and clothing, parasols and handmade quilts and rugs sharing space with early shaving mugs, razors, leather strops. Of particular interest is their collection of some 160 American pressed-glass goblets manufactured between 1830 and 1900, no two alike. The Schmincks willed the house and their collections to the Daughters of the American Revolution, who have recently renovated the building.

SCHMINCK MEMORIAL MUSEUM, 128 South E Street, Lakeview, OR 97630; (503) 947-3134.
Hours: 1–5 Tuesday–Saturday. Closed all holidays.
(Courtesy Oregon State Society of the Daughters of the American Revolution)

MOLALLA

HORACE DIBBLE HOUSE
1856–59

Molalla's oldest building is a striking departure in style from most Oregon homes of the period. By way of accounting for its classic New England saltbox architecture, the story goes that Horace Dibble engaged a former sea captain from the East Coast to build the house and gave him 320 acres of land in recompense for his three years' labor. Every board used in its six rooms was planed by hand. The house was furnished with period antiques, including some items made in Molalla. Noteworthy are two baskets woven by Mrs. Dibble under the tutelage of local Indian women. The pair of apple trees under which the Indians bartered smoked salmon and venison for the Dibbles' apples still stand in the garden. The Dibble House is owned by the Molalla Area Historical Association.

Folk arts and crafts are demonstrated at the Dibble House during Molalla's Annual Apple Festival in October. At that time the Frederick Vonder Ahe Home, an 1869 farmhouse also owned by the Molalla Area Historical Society, is opened to the public for the sale of down-home country victuals. Old-style fiddle players entertain.

HORACE DIBBLE HOUSE, 616 South Molalla Avenue, Molalla, OR 97038; (503) 829-8270.
Hours: June–September, 1–5 the second Sunday of the month. Also by appointment.
Admission fee.
(Courtesty Molalla Area Historical Association)

NEWBERG

THE HOOVER-MINTHORN HOUSE 1881

Between 1884 and 1889, this pleasant two-story Victorian frame house was the boyhood home of President Herbert Hoover. He was the nephew of Dr. Henry Minthorn, first superintendent of the Friends Pacific Academy and physician to Newberg's pioneer community, and Hoover had been invited to live with the Minthorns on the death of their only son in 1883. He shared their affectionate family life and attended the academy until he was fifteen, when Dr. Minthorn resigned and moved the family to Salem.

The Hoover-Minthorn House is now operated as a memorial to the former president, with many souvenirs and relics, among them his bedroom furniture. The pear tree in which he used to climb still grows in the garden.

THE HOOVER-MINTHORN HOUSE, 115 South River Street, Newberg, OR 97132; (503) 538-6629.

Hours: 1–4 Wednesday–Sunday. Tours by appointment.

Admission fee.

(Courtesy National Society of Colonial Dames of America in the State of Oregon)

OREGON CITY

McLOUGHLIN HOUSE NATIONAL HISTORIC SITE 1845–46

When Dr. John McLoughlin, a chief factor at the Hudson's Bay Company and founder of Oregon City, resigned his post in 1845, he built this Colonial-style home close to the Willamette River. The design is thought to be McLoughlin's and the materials to have come from the sawmill he had established in 1828 to produce timber for the Hawaiian Islands and the Spanish American trade.

McLoughlin was a dominant figure in the history of the Pacific Northwest. Born of an Irish Catholic father and a Scots Protestant mother in Quebec province in 1784, he grew to be a giant of a man with abilities and personal qualities to match. As chief factor of the Hudson's Bay Company's Columbia District, he administered a region extending from the Pacific Coast to the Rocky Mountains and from California to Alaska. His factorship was markedly successful: he expanded the company fur-trading activities to include agriculture, husbandry, and the export of lumber, salmon, and flour. In 1825 he established Fort Vancouver, and the tiny community that grew up around his sawmill near Willamette Falls became Oregon City in 1842. Throughout the period there were few uprisings among the Indians, who respectfully called him "White Eagle" for his shock of snow-white hair. But, sadly, his generosity to American settlers who had begun to settle Oregon Territory in 1834 ultimately worked to his detriment. His policies misunderstood, he resigned from the company and with his wife retired to their Oregon City property. There a small group of settlers managed to strip them of most of their claim. McLoughlin died brokenhearted in 1857.

McLoughlin House was moved to its present site in 1909. Today it is shown with many of McLoughlin's possessions and with appropriate period furnishings donated by various organizations. In 1970 the graves of Dr. and Mrs. McLoughlin were also moved to the site.

MCLOUGHLIN HOUSE NATIONAL HISTORIC SITE, 713 Center Street, Oregon City, OR 97045; (503) 656-5146.

Hours: Summer, 10–5 Tuesday–Sunday; winter, 11–4 Tuesday–Sunday. Closed January and holidays. Last tour an hour before closing time.

Admission fee.

(Courtesy McLoughlin Memorial Association and the National Park Service)

OREGON CITY

MERTIE STEVENS HOUSE MUSEUM 1907–08

This fifteen-room Georgian Revival house was a local pacesetter in its day, with such modern conveniences as radiators in each room and combination gas and electric chandeliers. Originally built by Harley C. Stevens, station agent for the Oregon Pacific Railroad, the house was deeded to the Clackamas County Historical Society in 1963 by Stevens's daughter, Mertie. It now serves as the Society's museum. The three-hundred-strong Sherlund Doll Collection is a notable feature.

MERTIE STEVENS HOUSE MUSEUM, Sixth and Washington streets, Oregon City, OR 97045; (503) 655-2866.
Hours: 1–5 Thursday and Sunday. Closed from Christmas week until February.
Admission fee.
(Courtesy Clackamas County Historical Society)

PORTLAND

PITTOCK MANSION
1909–14

Designed by San Francisco architect Edward L. Foulkes for Henry Pittock, founder of the *Daily Oregonian*, this enormous French Renaissance château commands a view of two states and two mountain peaks from its hilltop site. The house was built of reinforced concrete faced with Tenino sandstone to the most exacting standards of craftsmanship. It incorporated such pacesetting features as room-to-room telephones, a central vacuum-cleaning system, and an elevator to all floors. The principal rooms—remarkable for their plasterwork, cut and polished marble, and cast bronze—combine Victorian, Jacobean, and Georgian influences with the French Renaissance style. In the Turkish smoking room, the Tiffany wall glaze and ceiling paint are unretouched. But the furnishing most of us will remember is Henry Pittock's shower, designed to promote health as well as cleanliness. There is even a spigot for toe-testing the water temperature before entering the glass enclosure.

Long neglected, the Pittock Mansion was purchased by the city of Portland in 1964, restored, and refurnished with *objets d'art* and antiques loaned or donated by Pacific Northwest residents.

Pittock was seventy-three when he began the mansion. A self-made man (he had risen from printer's devil to publisher) with extensive business interests in other fields, he believed that young men should be given opportunities. Happily, several of the young craftsmen he entrusted to work on the mansion returned years later to supervise the restoration.

PITTOCK MANSION, 3229 Northwest Pittock Drive, Portland, OR 97210; (503) 248-4469.
Hours: Mid-June through Labor Day, 1–5 Tuesday–Friday; 12–5:30 Saturday and Sunday.
Admission fee.
(Courtesy City of Portland Bureau of Parks and Recreation)

ROSEBURG

LANE HOUSE
1853–54

John Creed Floed, son-in-law of Oregon Territory's first governor Gen. Joseph Lane, built this pleasant two-story frame house with fretwork balcony over the front porch. Although this house is often described as General Lane's home, the governor actually lived across the street in a small house constructed for him by the Floeds after his wife died. But Lane took all his meals with them and often whiled away the hours in their bay window facing Roseburg's new railway.

In 1959 General Lane's descendants deeded the house to the Douglas County Historical Society, which has refurbished the house with period antiques. A few of the Lane family's pieces remain.

LANE HOUSE, 554 Southeast Douglas Avenue, Roseburg, OR 97470; (503) 673-8175.
Hours: 1–5 Saturday and Sunday. Other times by appointment.
Admission by donation.
(Courtesy Douglas County Historical Society)

SALEM

BUSH HOUSE
1877–78

In the period 1877–78, Asahel Bush II, banker, official state printer, and founder of the *Oregon Statesman,* commissioned Wilbur F. Boothy to design a large mansion in the Italianate style on his Salem estate. Its interiors combine the principles of beauty and utility Bush felt were so important—choice furnishings, wallpapers imported from France, Italian marble fireplaces, and the most modern conveniences available at the time.

An elegantly crafted walnut and mahogany staircase is a feature of the twelve rooms open to the public today. Most of the furnishings belonged to the Bush family, who occupied the house for seventy-five years. Bush House is surrounded by a lovely park that formerly was pasture for the estate cattle. The barn now serves as a community art center.

BUSH HOUSE, 600 Mission Street S.E., Salem, OR 97301; (503) 363-4714.
Hours: September–May, 2–5 Tuesday–Sunday; June–August, 12–5 Tuesday–Sunday.
Admission fee.
(Courtesy Salem Art Association)

SALEM

DEEPWOOD HOUSE
1894–95

The plans for Dr. Luke A. Port's new residence on a six-acre tract in Yew Park attracted a good deal of attention in the Salem press at the time. And rightly so. The site was beautiful, with a living spring, grass, and a forest, and would be improved with an artificial lake. Stylistically, the house would be in the fashionable Queen Anne manner, with two stories, a basement, and a cupola, and it was to be supplied with every convenience known to the house-builders of the day. Port, an English immigrant who had served in the Union army during the Civil War, commissioned Oregon's future state architect, W. C. Knighton, to draw up the plans. When Deepwood was completed, it was considered one of the handsomest homes in Oregon.

Deepwood has been attractively refurbished recently with donated furnishings. Particularly striking features are the eastern-oak woodwork and the Italian art glass by Povey Brothers of Portland, Oregon; over the fireplace is a memorial window to one of the Port children. A large carriage house designed by Knighton to complement the house and an ironwork gazebo from Portland's 1905 Lewis and Clark Exposition are prominent among the outbuildings.

Deepwood was successively home to four families after Dr. Port sold it to the George Bingham family in 1895. Today it serves as a community center as much as a house museum.

DEEPWOOD HOUSE, 1116 Mission Street S.E., Salem, OR 97301; (503) 363-1825.
Hours: April–September, 1:30–4:30 Tuesday–Friday, Sunday, and the second Saturday of each month; October–March, 1:30–4:30 Wednesday, Friday, and Sunday.
Admission fee.
(Courtesy The Friends of Deepwood)

SALEM

MISSION MILL MUSEUM

In a quiet park near Willamette University stands the Mission Mill Museum complex. The complex preserves four structures of importance in Oregon's early history, among them the home of the Rev. Jason Lee, the missionary chosen to establish the Methodist church in the Northwest. His decision to establish the mission on the banks of the Willamette River contributed to the development of the Chemekitty area into Salem; he also helped inspire the Great Emigration to Oregon in 1842. He stands with Dr. John McLoughlin of the Hudson's Bay Company as one who shaped the future of the Pacific Northwest.

Boon House

1847

This two-story house was Salem's first single-family dwelling. It was the home of John D. Boon, who came to Oregon Territory in 1847, held posts in Oregon's first three governments, served as a probate judge, and partnered Joseph Watts in establishing Salem's first woollen mill. None of the furniture in the house is orginal to Boon's day, but most is typical of the period and includes a sea chest from the famous battleship, *Old Ironsides.*

Lee House

1841

Like its neighbor the Parsonage (see below), Lee House is thought to be one of the oldest structures built by white men in the Northwest Territory. It was certainly the region's first mission house. Of frame construction, it was divided into four small "apartments" where families lived separately; with their many original furnishings, the apartments vividly evoke early frontier life. The apartment on the ground floor was occupied for a period by Jason Lee and his second wife, Lucy Thomson Lee.

The Parsonage

1841

Designed by Hamilton Campbell of the Mission staff, this tongue-and-groove house with outside stair was built in the fall of 1841 as the mission's Indian manual training school. Later, the second floor was used to house mission mill laborers without families. The Parsonage contains among its furnishings the dining room furniture of Dr. John McLoughlin, founder of Oregon City and a chief factor of the Hudson's Bay Company. McLoughlin's home in Oregon City is now a national monument and open to the public.

MISSION MILL MUSEUM, 260 12th Street S.E., Salem, OR 97301; (503) 585-7012.

Hours: June–October, 1:30–4:30 Wednesday–Sunday. November–May, 1:30–4:30 Wednesday and Sunday.

(Courtesy Mission Mill Museum)

SAUVIE ISLAND

BYBEE-HOWELL HOUSE
1856

Set well back from the water on a knoll affording views across Multnomah Channel toward the Tualatins, Bybee-Howell House is the last survivor of Sauvie Island's earliest farmsteads. It was built by Col. James F. Bybee, a Kentucky horsebreeder who had struck it rich enough in the California goldfields to build a substantial nine-room home for his family and a straightaway track for his thoroughbreds. Unable to support his title "King of the Oregon Turf," Bybee sold out to his neighbors, Dr. Benjamin Howell and his wife Elizabeth, in 1858. The house remained in the Howell family until 1959, when it was acquired by Multnomah County, forming the nucleus of a historical and natural conservancy known as Howell Territorial Park.

The Bybee-Howell House, in the Greek Revival style, re-creates the ambience of the 1850s both indoors and out. The gardens contain ancient roses and a collection of native Oregon flora as well as some of the original pear and cherry trees, now over a century old. Of particular interest is the Oregon Pioneer orchard, preserving from extinction about 160 different old varieties of fruit trees that date back to Oregon's beginnings. Near the houe is the Agricultural Museum, guide staffed and open at house hours.

BYBEE-HOWELL HOUSE, 13901 Northwest Howell Park Road, Sauvie Island, OR 97231; (503) 621-3344.

Hours: June–August, 12–5; also open last weekend in September. Schedule subject to annual change.

(Courtesy Oregon Historical Society)

SILVERTON

AMES-WARNOCK HOUSE (Silverton Country Museum) 1908

Moved to its present location in 1975, this turn-of-the-century home now houses the Silverton Country Museum. The interior has changed little. Three rooms on the main floor re-create an early twentieth century parlor, dining room, and bedroom with period furnishings; a fourth room replicates a one-room school; and another a kitchen. Also displayed is a collection of political cartoons by Homer Davenport and Frank Bower, former cartoonists for the Hearst chain of newspapers.

AMES-WARNOCK HOUSE, 428 South Water Street, Silverton, OR 97381; (503) 873-3534.
Hours: 1–4 Thursday and Sunday; other times by appointment.
Admission by donation.
(Courtesy Silverton Country Museum)

WOODBURN

SETTLEMIER HOUSE
1889

When Jesse Settlemier platted four blocks of his nursery land beside the Oregon Central's new track in 1871, and then compounded his lunacy by offering free lots to anyone who would put up a building, the trappers of French Prairie thought it the best joke of the year. But the young nurseryman from Oregon City enjoyed the last laugh; by 1878 the town of Woodburn boasted a population of 145, a church, a school, a lodge, and a general-merchandise store, and its civic future looked bright.

Ever an astute businessman, Settlemier built up one of the largest nurseries west of the Mississippi, supplying stock to the entire West, from British Columbia to Mexico. He also served his community, as Woodburn's first mayor and member of the state legislature.

The handsome fourteen-room Queen Anne–style mansion built by Settlemier and his third wife, Mary C. Woodworth, is shown with period furnishings that include some of the original family pieces. The garden has a few of the trees from Settlemier's original nursery stock.

SETTLEMIER HOUSE, 355 North Settlemier Avenue, Woodburn, OR 97071; (503) 982-9363.
Hours: Winter, 1–4 Sunday; summer, 1–5 Sunday. Closed January.
Admission fee.
(Courtesy French Prairie Historical Association)

WASHINGTON

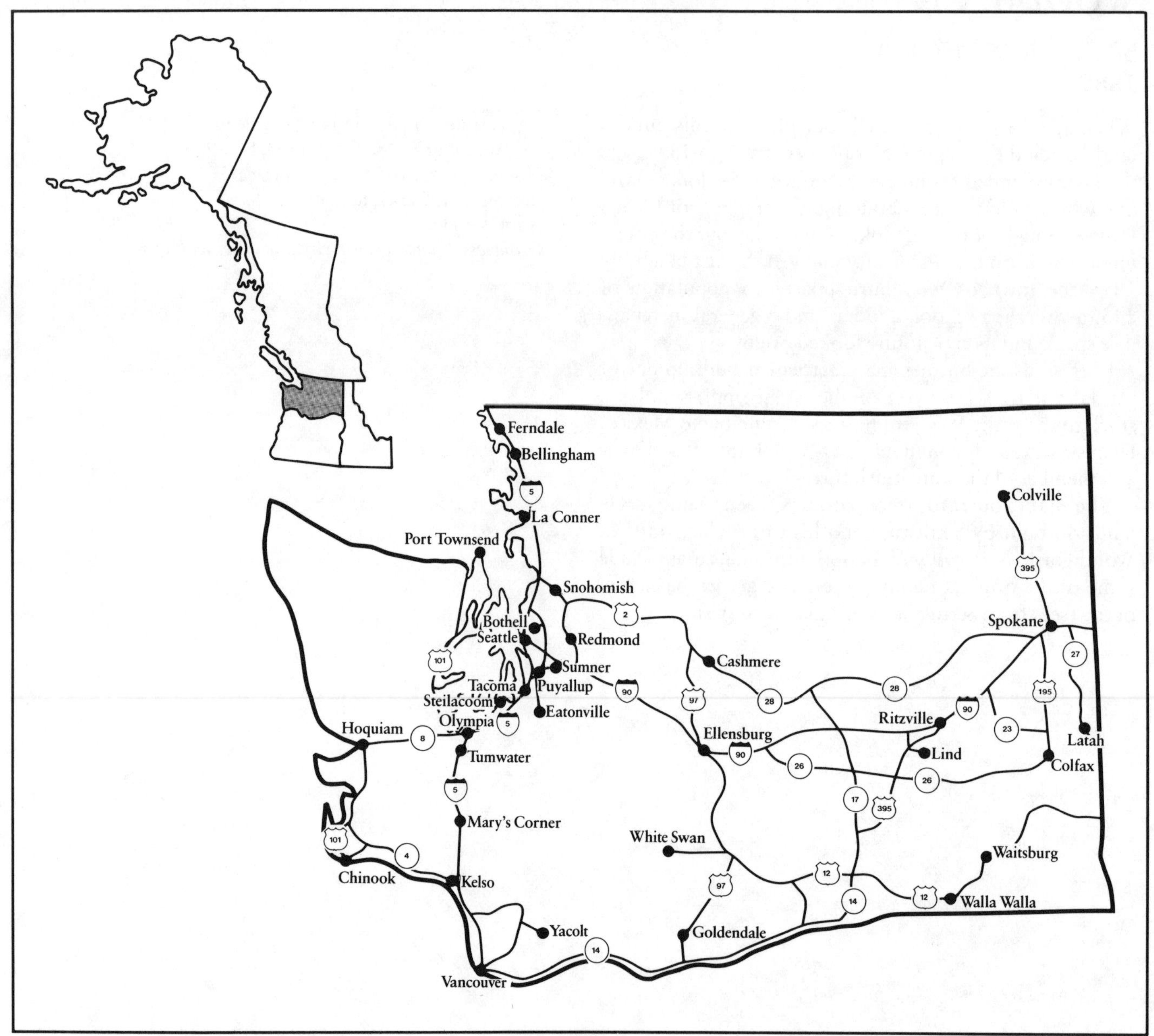
Ferndale
Bellingham
La Conner
Port Townsend
Snohomish
Bothell
Seattle
Redmond
Sumner
Tacoma
Puyallup
Steilacoom
Eatonville
Olympia
Hoquiam
Tumwater
Mary's Corner
Chinook
Kelso
Yacolt
Vancouver
Colville
Spokane
Cashmere
Ritzville
Ellensburg
Lind
Latah
Colfax
White Swan
Waitsburg
Walla Walla
Goldendale
5
101
2
90
97
28
8
27
195
23
26
17
395
4
12
14

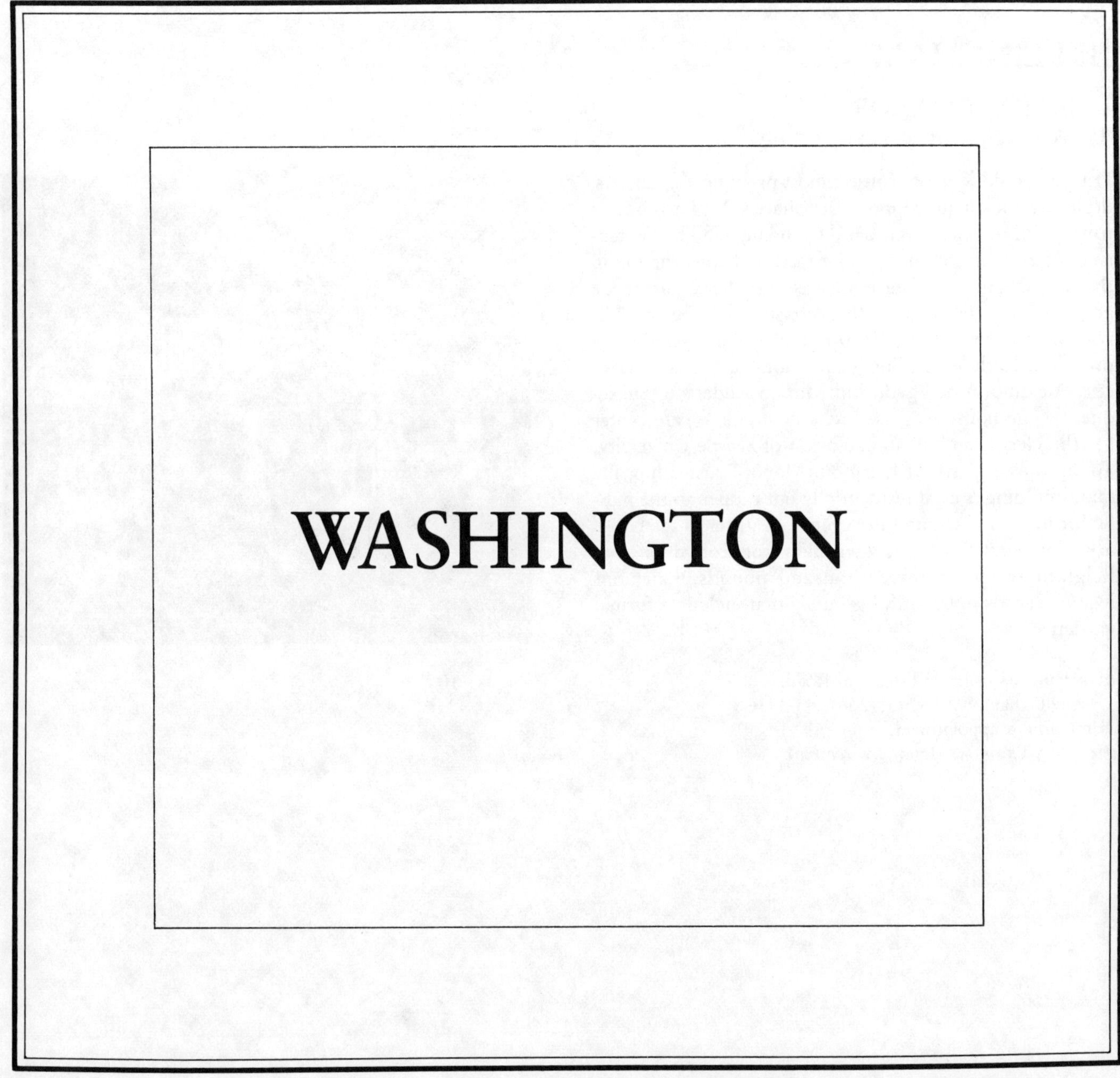

WASHINGTON

BELLINGHAM

LAIRMONT MANOR
1916

Francis Gould, one of Seattle's most prominent architects, designed Lairmont Manor for Charles X. Larrabee, a founder of the Fairhaven Land Company who had extensive interests in shipping, real estate, and construction in the Bellingham area. Lairmont was to evidence Larrabee's great wealth. He died before construction began. His widow completed the $150,000 house and resided there until her death, entertaining such notable guests as Princess Alexandria of Egypt and Marian Anderson. Subsequently the house was used as a novitiate, a care center for the clergy, and as an extension of Seattle University. Today the property of Lairmont Manor Trusteeship, the main building is used residentially but is open to the public for tours and community events. Features of the house are inlaid wall panels and a wrought-iron front door from Belgium weighing three thousand pounds. Lairmont Manor stands in beautiful grounds that include a formal garden.

LAIRMONT MANOR, 405 Fieldstone Road,
Bellingham, WA 98225; (206) 743-3536.
Admission by appointment.
(Courtesy Lairmont Manor Trusteeship)

BELLINGHAM

PICKETT HOUSE
1856

When Capt. George E. Pickett of the U.S. Army came to Washington's Whatcom County during the Indian wars in the 1850s to build Fort Bellingham, he also constructed this small house as a home for himself and his Indian bride, a Haida noblewoman. (Pickett was later to achieve enduring fame as leader of the Confederate charge at Gettysburg that changed the course of the Civil War.)

In Pickett's day, the main part of the house consisted of a study and a master bedroom downstairs and two upstairs bedrooms that were reached by a ladder. A lean-to at the side of the house was used as dining room and kitchen; it's said that cougars would warm themselves on its roof during the winter months. Over the years renovations were made by various owners to make the house more livable. It is now the museum and meetinghouse of the Whatcom County Daughters of the Pioneers, containing mementoes of Captain Pickett and early Whatcom County. A pear tree planted by Pickett in 1856 still blooms in the backyard.

PICKETT HOUSE, 910 Bancroft Street (between E and F streets), Bellingham, WA 98225.
Hours: 1–5 Sunday.
(Courtesy Whatcom County Daughters of the Pioneers, Chapter 5)

BELLINGHAM

ROEDER HOME
1903

Victor Roeder, a son of one of Bellingham's founders, began building this large Craftsman home in 1903. He commissioned a leading local architect, Alfred Lee, and spared no expense; when the house was completed in 1908 it boasted a built-in vacuum system, hand-painted murals, and fine oak paneling among its elegances. A feature of the house is a late medieval style staircase with carved urns crowning the newel posts.

Roeder managed the family business as well as the Bellingham National Bank, which he started in 1904, and from 1896 to 1900 he also served as Whatcom County's treasurer. In 1926 he subdivided his property so that his daughter Ayreness and son-in-law Russell could build a home. You may still see the weights and measurements of all the Roeder children and grandchildren recorded on a door frame in the basement of the Roeder home.

Donated to the Whatcom County Park Board in 1971, the house is now a community cultural and educational center. It is being restored to the Roeders' period and retains some of their original furniture and some handsome brass light fixtures with Steuben glass shades.

ROEDER HOME, 2600 Sunset Drive, Bellingham, WA 98226; (206) 733-6897.
Tours by appointment.
(Courtesy Whatcom County Park and Recreation Board)

BOTHELL

BOTHELL HISTORICAL MUSEUM (William Hannan House) 1893

Moved from its original Main Street site, this two-story house built by Bothell's former postmaster William Hannan has been situated in an attractive historical park on the Sammamish River. It now serves as a museum of turn-of-the-century items. Also of interest is the nearby *Beckstrom Log Cabin* (1885), which once housed a family of ten.

BOTHELL HISTORICAL MUSEUM, 9919 Northeast 180th, Bothell, WA 98011; (206) 486-1889.
Hours: 1–4 Sunday. Closed Easter and Mother's Day.
(Courtesy Bothell Historical Museum Society)

CASHMERE

CHELAN COUNTY HISTORICAL SOCIETY PIONEER VILLAGE AND HISTORICAL MUSEUM

More than twenty pioneer buildings constructed in Chelan County from 1870 to 1905 have been moved here to form Chelan County Historical Society's Pioneer Village, among them a blacksmith shop, a post office, a saloon, and several log homes. The *Richardson Cabin* (1888), built at Monitor of fir logs cut at Horseshoe Lake and skidded to the homesite, has been restored and furnished as a memorial to all the early Chelan County settlers. The *Weymouth Cabin* (1891) is a "board and batten" frame structure of rough-sawn lumber typical of early settler homes in the area. There is also a replica of the log *Mission* established near Cashmere between 1856 and 1863 by the Oblate Fathers (possibly by Father Pandosy, who later founded the mission at Kelowna, British Columbia). The original buildings were put up on the banks of the stream now called Mission Creek, some three-quarters of a mile south of Cashmere's present city limits. The *Chelan County Historical Museum* features the Willis Carey collection of Indian artifacts and pioneer relics.

CHELAN COUNTY HISTORICAL SOCIETY PIONEER VILLAGE AND HISTORICAL MUSEUM, 105 Parkhill Street, Cashmere, WA 98815; (509) 782-3230.
Hours: 10–5 daily in summer.
(Courtesy Chelan County Historical Society)

CHINOOK

FORT COLUMBIA STATE PARK
1895–1902

Fort Columbia was a coastal artillery fort, built, with Forts Canby and Stevens, to guard the mouth of the Columbia River. It is a peaceful place, converted now to peaceful purposes. There are batteries on Chinook Point, installed between 1896 and 1898, that never fired a shot in anger. The turn-of-the-century buildings that housed the garrison until World War II now do duty, among other things, as museums, a theater, and a youth hostel. The former *Enlisted Men's Barracks* is now used as the park interpretive center. Largely restored and refurnished to the period 1902, the building houses a squad room complete with beds and wall lockers, a kitchen with three coal-fired ranges, and wall displays featuring the history of exploration of the area. In the old *Commandant's Quarters* you will find a Daughters of the American Revolution museum depicting life in the fort.

FORT COLUMBIA STATE PARK, P.O Box 236, Chinook, WA 98614; (206) 777-8221 or 777-8358. The fort is located on U.S. Highway 101, one mile east of Chinook.
Hours: Open daily April 2–October 14, 6–10; October 15–April 1, 8–5.
(Courtesy Washington State Parks and Recreation Commission)

COLFAX

PERKINS HOUSE
1884

Sharing a tree-shaded lot are the original homestead cabin and late-Victorian home of James Ellis Perkins, one of the founders of Colfax. Perkins and his partner Thomas Smith arrived in the Colfax area in the summer of 1870 to establish a sawmill at the junction of the Palouse River forks. Their cabin was built with lumber and logs hauled from Walla Walla, however. It was so lonely a life that one of the men caught a mouse for company and kept it tethered with a string. Smith soon abandoned the project, and it was with a new partner, Hezekiah Stout Hollingsworth, that Perkins surveyed the townsite that became Colfax and nursed it into a flourishing little community boasting over fifty businesses by 1880. He served four times as mayor and counted the Bank of Colfax among his many business interests.

Perkins built a two-story house with gingerbread scrollwork and four balconies to accommodate his growing family between 1884 and 1886. Acquired by the Whitman County Historical Society in 1973, it has been restored to its appearance in the 1880s and refurnished in the style characteristic of eastern Washington families of the Perkinses' period and economic standing.

PERKINS HOUSE, 623 Perkins Avenue, Colfax, WA 99111.
Hours: 1–4 Thursday and Saturday.
(Courtesy Whitman County Historical Society)

COLVILLE

KELLER HOUSE
1910

Keller House has been the home of two of Colville's prominent businessmen. Its builder, J. H. Young, was operating a stagecoach line in 1885 when news of a silver strike in the hills north of Colville reached Spokane. He seized the opportunity to provide transportation for the miners (his livery stable and stage service became one of Colville's first businesses) and cannily invested in a number of business ventures. Eventual sale of his interest in one mine alone realized him more than a million dollars. In 1910 Young commissioned one of Spokane's leading architects, Loren L. Rand, to design this spacious Craftsman-style home as an elegant capstone to his success.

Young's widow Anna married Louis G. Keller in 1915. Son of a successful Cincinnati merchant with hardware stores in California and Florida, Keller laid the foundations of his own wealth by opening a hardware store in Colville in 1907. Like "Harry" Young, he played a prominent role in Colville's growth from a rough-and-tumble mining town to an important commercial center. He bequeathed Keller House to the city. Unaltered and with its beautifully crafted Arts and Crafts decoration intact, the house is shown with period furnishings. Particularly notable are the leaded and beveled glass windows and painted walls in the dining room.

On the grounds are the Stevens County Historical Museum, a carriage house, and Colville's first schoolhouse. These three structures, along with Keller House, offer a rounded portrait of the county's history.

KELLER HOUSE, Keller Historical Park,
700 North Wynne Street, Colville,
WA 99114; (509) 684-5968.
Open May 1–September 30. Call for hours.
(Courtesy Stevens County Historical Society)

EATONVILLE

DOVE CENTER PIONEER FARM MUSEUM

This unusual museum offers a participatory experience in pioneer history as well as a chance to tour authentic pioneer-era structures on a thirty-acre estate near Eatonville. At present just one program is available to the general public (others are for school groups); dressed in pioneer garb and using pioneer tools, participants perform such tasks as peeling logs, milking a cow, churning butter, and scrubbing clothes just as the early settlers did. The buildings include a trading post, a pole barn, two cabins, a blacksmith shop, and a wood shop. The trading post is an 1890s hand-hewn log cabin originally located at Cranberry Lake and owned by a fur trapper neamed Robert S. McClimans.

DOVE CENTER PIONEER FARM MUSEUM,
P.O. Box 35/Route 3, Eatonville, WA 98328;
(206) 832-6300.
Call for hours.
(Courtesy The Development of the Ohop Valley for Education Center Pioneer Farm Museum)

ELLENSBURG

OLMSTEAD PLACE STATE PARK
1875

Olmstead Place State Historical Park offers a lively and instructive look at the Kittitas Valley's past, with old buildings maintained as a "living historical farm" where pioneer techniques—from butter churning to spinning—are demonstrated. The 217-acre ranch was homesteaded in 1875 by Samuel Bedient Olmstead, descendant of a founder of Hartford, Connecticut, and was farmed by his family for nearly a century. In 1968 his granddaughters deeded the ranch to the state of Washington as a heritage site.

Log Cabin
1875

This is the original Olmstead home, built by Samuel of hand-hewn cottonwood logs taken from a nearby canyon. These were pegged together and chinked with mud, dry wild grass, and horsehair. Furnished in typical pioneer fashion, the cabin is surrounded by a garden with period plantings that include berry bushes and fruit trees brought by freight wagon from an Oregon nursery before 1880.

Olmstead Residence
1908

Twenty-six years after Samuel's death in 1882, his wife Sarah and their sons and their families moved into this wood frame house with a cedar shingle roof. It was the family residence until 1981, when the last granddaughter died.

Red Barn
1908

Built to store grain and hay, the barn now houses a collection of historic farm implements and machinery.

Seaton Cabin
Ca. 1876

One of the Olmsteads recalled that this log cabin was built by a Kittitas Valley homesteader, S. T. Sterling, more than a century ago. For some years after 1876 the building served as a home as well as a schoolhouse where children of pioneer families learned the three Rs from a Pennsylvanian schoolteacher, Mrs. Charles Terry. In the 1940s the cabin was acquired by the Seaton family, who donated it to the state.

OLMSTEAD PLACE STATE PARK, P.O. Box 2580/ Route 5 (3½ miles east of Ellensburg on Old Squaw Creek Trail Road), Ellensburg, WA 98926; (509) 925-1943.

Hours: May–September, 8–5 daily; tours daily. October–April, by appointment.

(Courtesy Washington State Parks and Recreation Commission)

FERNDALE

HOVANDER HOMESTEAD 1903 NIELSEN HOUSE (TENNANT LAKE NATURAL HISTORY CENTER) 1906

These two homes, very different in style, are located in the outskirts of Ferndale between the Nooksack River and Tennant Lake. They were built on land cleared in 1858 by the area's first settlers, John and Clara Tennant. Toward the turn of the century the property came into possession of the Nielsen family, who in turn sold some sixty acres to a retired Swedish architect, Holan Hovander. Hovander built a large and elegant home overlooking the river, and three years later the Nielsens completed their home near Tennant Lake. Both homes were family occupied until the 1970s, when they were purchased by Whatcom County Park and Recreation Board to form a new park that, with Tennant Lake, offers architectural as well as natural history.

The *Hovander Homestead* (1903), regarded as a fine example of a turn-of-the-century wood-frame home in the Stick style, is furnished with a large collection of Swedish antiques. Hovander himself laid all the brick, helped by his children, who mixed river sand with the mortar. On the grounds is a large red barn built in 1911 that houses a collection of early farm implements, a children's farm zoo, and picnicking facilities. A trail leads from the house beside the slough to the former Nielsen home, now the park's natural-history interpretive center, where exhibits and programs promote understanding of Tennant Lake's abundant wildlife.

HOVANDER HOMESTEAD-TENNANT LAKE NATURAL HISTORY CENTER, Ferndale, WA 98248. To get to Tennant Lake Natural History Interpretive Center from Ferndale, go south on Hovander Road to Nielsen Road. Continue to River Lea Road for Hovander Homestead.

Hours: Park: Open daily 10–dusk. Hovander House: Open daily in summer; by appointment rest of year. For information on hours and tours, call the park manager, (206) 384-3444. Tennant Lake Interpretive Center: Open Wednesday–Sunday, year round. For information on programs, hours, tours, call the interpretive naturalist, (206) 384-5545.

(Courtesy Whatcom County Park and Recreation Board)

GOLDENDALE

KLICKITAT COUNTY HISTORICAL MUSEUM (William Presby Mansion) 1902

Built by attorney William B. Presby, this twenty-room mansion in the Queen Anne style is, with the exception of its interior decoration, in its original state. Now a local-history museum, it is furnished with antiques and relics used in the area during the last century and a quarter. Among them is a collection of 115 coffee mills and more than 300 Klickitat County cattle brands on leather patches.

KLICKITAT COUNTY HISTORICAL MUSEUM, 127 West Broadway, Goldendale, WA 98620; (509) 773-4303.
Hours: May1 –October 15, 8–5 Tuesday–Sunday; at other times by appointment.
Admission fee.
(Courtesy Klickitat County Historical Society)

GOLDENDALE

MARYHILL MUSEUM OF ART
1914–22

Situated on a plateau overlooking the Columbia River, the imposing building that is now Maryhill Museum recalls the idealistic plans of Seattle lawyer and philanthropist Sam Hill for an agricultural colony he called "The Promised Land."

Hill was one of those larger-than-life personalities who crop up so often in the history of the Pacific Northwest. Born of an old Quaker family in Deep River, North Carolina, he brought, a friend remembered, "a great ambition to do good in the world" as well as a formidable intellect and unflagging energy to his many business interests. He had made his fortune as president of several companies in the empire of railroad magnate James J. Hill before moving to Seattle at the end of the century.

In 1907, the story goes, Hill's speculations about an ideal agricultural zone where western rains and eastern sunshine met seemed realized among the hills near Goldendale. He purchased nearly seven thousand acres, hoping to attract Quakers who would help him make the desert bloom. A road, a hotel, and several houses were constructed before it was clear that the dream was his alone. Hill then commissioned the architects Hornblower and Marshall to design a grand mansion for the site; later, influenced by the dancer Loie Fuller, he decided to make his new home a museum "for the betterment of French art in the Far Northwest of America." The museum was dedicated by Hill's friend, Queen Marie of Romania, in 1926.

Maryhill Museum's collections were developed with the help of Alma de Bretteville Spreckels, donor of San Francisco's California Palace of the Legion of Honor. They include distinguished works by Auguste Rodin and Emil Galle. One gallery is devoted to memorabilia and furniture that belonged to Queen Marie. Upriver, not far from the museum, Hill erected a concrete model of England's great prehistoric monument, Stonehenge, his memorial to those who fell in World War I. A path leads from the momument to his grave.

MARYHILL MUSEUM OF ART, P.O. Box 23/
Star Route 677, Goldendale, WA 98620;
(509) 773-4729.
Hours: March 15–November 15, 9–5 daily.
Admission fee.
(Courtesy Maryhill Museum of Art)

HOQUIAM

HOQUIAM'S CASTLE
1897

Lumber baron Robert Lytle built this twenty-room mansion with Richardsonian influences far above the hurly-burly of Hoquiam's sawmills. Restored and furnished by the Robert Watson family in 1971, the house is enhanced by late-Victorian and Edwardian antiques that include a six-hundred-piece cut crystal chandelier in the main parlor. The third-floor ballroom opens onto an open-air deck affording a sweeping panorama of the city and Grays Harbor.

HOQUIAM'S CASTLE, 515 Chenault Avenue,
Hoquiam, WA 98550; (206) 533-2005.
Hours: Summer, 11–5 daily; rest of the year, by appointment.
Admission fee.
(Courtesy Mrs. and Mrs. Robert Watson)

HOQIUAM

POLSON MUSEUM HOUSE
1923

This twenty-six-room Colonial Revival house was designed by the prominent Seattle architect Arthur Loveless for Arnold and Priscilla Polson, both members of pioneer Grays Harbor lumber families. The site was part of property purchased by Arnold's father, Alan Polson, in 1890, and the old family home stood where the present rose garden is located.

As the Polson family owned seventeen logging camps and a sawmill, the finest materials for the house came readily to hand. An unusual feature of the interior is the hemlock flooring; unbroken lengths of wood, some pieces thirty-two feet long, were used.

Polson House was donated to the city of Hoquiam in 1976 as a memorial to Arnold Polson. It is used as a local history museum of Grays Harbor County, featuring displays of logging and sawmill pictures and equipment.

POLSON MUSEUM HOUSE, 1611 Riverside Avenue, Hoquiam, WA 98550; (206) 533-5862.
Hours: June–August, 12–4 daily; September–May, 12–4 Saturday and Sunday.
(Courtesy Polson Park and Museum Historical Society)

KELSO

COWLITZ COUNTY HISTORICAL MUSEUM
Ben's Cabin (1884)
Bush Cabin (1863)

Preserved on the Cowlitz County Historical Museum premises is the split-log cabin built near the Toutle River by Ben Beagle in 1884. Beagle, a Pennsylvanian, came to Washington Territory in the 1880s with his brother and three sisters. He remained a bachelor all his life, living in this small cabin and working at many trades. He farmed his own land, worked in shingle bolt camps, cruised timber, and for a time mined copper in the St. Helen's area. Early pioneers recalled him as a good friend and neighbor, a great reader, and a striking figure of a man who stood over six feet tall and sported a full beard. His cabin is furnished with period artifacts.

Bush Cabin, built in 1863, was originally located north of Longview in the Hazel Dell district. It was the first home of Edgar C. and Catherine Bush, early donation-land settlers in Cowlitz County. The cabin was acquired by the Cowlitz County Historical Society in 1953 and moved to its present site at the Cowlitz County fairgrounds.

COWLITZ COUNTY HISTORICAL MUSEUM, 405 Allen Street, Kelso, WA 98626; (206) 577-3119.
Hours: 1–5 Tuesday–Sunday.
(Courtesy Cowlitz County Historical Museum)

LaCONNER

GACHES MANSION
1891

This imposing Tudoresque mansion was built by George Gaches and his wife Louisa in 1891. When the Gaches came to LaConner from England they occupied a smaller, much more modest home built on the site in 1883. George, in partnership with his brother James, purchased a dry goods store from John and Louisa Conner and began the first shipments of hay and grains from the Winomis flats; by 1891 he could afford to build his homesick wife a proper English mansion so that she would feel more at home in her adopted country.

After the Gaches moved to Seattle in 1900 the mansion passed through several hands. It was used by Dr. G. E. Howe as a hospital, then sold by him to the L. W. Vaughan family, who lived there until the mid-1930s. From 1940 until fire destroyed the third floor in 1973, the mansion was used as an apartment and rooming house.

The Gaches Mansion is now owned by LaConner Landmarks, a nonprofit organization. It has been restored and redecorated in keeping with its turn-of-the-century architectural style. The period furnishings have been donated by Skagit Valley families. The second floor serves as the Valley Museum of Northwest Art, exhibiting the work of such major Northwest painters as Mark Tobey, Morris Graves, and Guy Anderson.

GACHES MANSION, P.O. Box 692/602 South Second, LaConner, WA 98257; (206) 466-4288. Museum, (206) 466-4445 or 466-3033.
Hours: April–September, 1–5 Friday, Saturday, Sunday; October–December and February–March, 1–4 Saturday, Sunday. Closed January.
Admission fee.
(Courtesy LaConner Landmarks)

LATAH

HAM-McEACHERN HOUSE
Ca. 1886

Occupying four large lots on the corner of Pine and Fifth streets in the wheat town of Latah is the Queen Anne–style Ham-McEachern House built about 1886 by David T. Ham, co-founder of Latah's first store and one of Washington's most influential political and business leaders in the early years of the twentieth century. In 1905 Ham sold the house to William A. McEachern, founder of the Bank of Latah. McEacherns have lived there ever since. As a consequence the interior reflects the tastes and interests of one family over a period of some eighty years. Among the family portraits is a painting of Flora McDonald, the Scottish Jacobite heroine who helped Bonnie Prince Charles escape from Scotland after his defeat at Culloden in 1746. Flora was a McEachern cousin.

HAM-MCEACHERN HOUSE, Pine and Fifth streets, Latah, WA 99018; (509) 286-3563.
Open in summer by appointment.
(Courtesy Almeda McEachern Oatman)

LIND

SEIVERS BROTHERS RANCH HOUSE AND BARN
1908

In a sheltered hollow amid the wheat fields southeast of Lind is the turn-of-the-century home of a pioneer wheat-farming family that settled in the area over a century ago. The Seivers brothers, Nicholas and Peter, arrived in Adams County in 1882. Their homestead cabin and first ranch-house have been succeeded by the present twenty-five room structure, constructed between 1908 and 1910, which features an encircling verandah, fifteen bedrooms, a ballroom, and family furniture and memorabilia handed down over three generations.

The large two-story barn across the farmyard was designed and constructed for the Seivers brothers in 1905 by a retired shipwright, P. Barnum. His craftsmanship was of high order—not a nail was used in the support timbers. Measuring 60 feet by 120 feet, it could house as many as fifty-eight horses or mules as well as the tons of feed they required. Barnum's tool chest may still be seen.

The Seivers Ranch is still owned, operated, and occupied by descendants of Nicholas and Peter Seivers. Visitors are requested to call in advance for an appointment to see the property.

SEIVERS BROTHERS RANCH HOUSE AND BARN,
Providence Road, Lind, WA 99341;
(509) 677-3625.
Admission by appointment only.
(Courtesy Nick Seivers)

MARY'S CORNER

JOHN R. JACKSON HOUSE
1845

This log cabin is thought to be the first American pioneer home built north of the Columbia River, and the U.S. District Court convened there several times after November 1850. It was built by John Robinson Jackson, a native of County Durham, England, who had farmed in Illinois for ten years before migrating west in 1844. In 1847 he enlarged the cabin to accommodate his bride, Matilda Glover Koontz, and a ready-made family of four boys, her sons by her first marriage. Its glass windows, split-cedar floor and staircase were luxurious by pioneer standards.

Jackson combined many callings in his life—justice of the peace, court clerk, tax assessor and collector, sheriff, postmaster—and used the cabin as home, inn, and general store. Among the famous who enjoyed his hospitality were Generals Ulysses S. Grant, Sheridan, and McClellan.

At present the cabin is closed to visitors, but you may view the interior through the windows. Most of the furnishings that you can see belonged to the Jackson family.

JOHN R. JACKSON HOUSE, US 12, Mary's Corner (seven miles south of Chehalis), WA 98532.
(Courtesy Washington State Parks and Recreation Commission)

OLYMPIA

BIGELOW HOUSE
1854

The story of Bigelow House may be said to begin in 1850 in Belleville, New York. There Daniel R. Bigelow, a young Harvard-trained lawyer who thought he was going to go blind, decided to join a wagon train to Portland, Oregon, to see the West before he did. He sailed on to Olympia a year later. The future state capital was then only a huddle of some three dozen cabins and Indian huts, but Bigelow opened a law office and took out a 350-acre land grant for a farm on the eastern slopes of Bud Inlet.

Bigelow never did lose his sight, and he was prominent in local affairs all his long life. His public career included service as a code commissioner revising laws for the new Washington Territory in 1853 and as a state legislator for several terms. He supported legislation that permitted women to vote in the state elections in 1884 and 1886. He died in 1905 at the age of eighty-one.

Bigelow House was built in the summer of 1854 after Daniel's marriage to Elizabeth White, the area's first schoolteacher. It is a charming example of a small Gothic Revival home, retaining its original stables and woodshed; considerably altered over the years, it now stands on a fraction of the former land grant, enclosed by a black iron fence. Direct descendants of David and Elizabeth still live there, surrounded by many of their possessions, some of which were shipped around the Horn in the 1850s and 1860s. Among them is Daniel's imposing rolltop desk.

BIGELOW HOUSE, 918 Glass Avenue, Olympia, WA 98506; (206) 357-6198.
Admission by appintment only. At least three day's notice required.
(Courtesy Mr. and Mrs. Daniel S. Bigelow)

OLYMPIA

STATE CAPITOL MUSEUM (C. J. Lord Mansion) Ca. 1920

Designed by local architect Joseph Wohleb for Clarence J. Lord, a former president of the Capitol National Bank, and his wife Mary, this stucco mansion in the Spanish Renaissance style now houses a museum of Pacific Northwest history. The house originally contained thirty-two rooms on three floors, many of them paneled with such choice woods as Brazilian mahogany and pecan. The gardens were laid out by Fred Cole, who obtained his training at London's Kew Gardens. Today the grounds include a native plant garden and a pioneer herb garden. (The herbs are dried, packaged, and sold in the museum's gift shop.)

STATE CAPITOL MUSEUM, 211 West 21st Avenue, Olympia, WA 98501; (206) 753-2580.
Hours: 10–4 Tuesday–Friday; 12–4 Saturday and Sunday. Closed state holidays.
(Courtesy State Capitol Museum)

PORT TOWNSEND

FORT WORDEN STATE PARK (Commander's House) 1904

Formerly headquarters of the Harbor Defenses of Puget Sound, Fort Worden is regarded as an excellent example of turn-of-the-century military construction in the West. The 2½-story Commander's House, its architectural style similar to Jeffersonian Classicism, has been refurbished as a museum to illustrate a Victorian dwelling and to show how commanding officers lived during that era. The furnishings of each room represent a different style, ranging from 1830 to 1910.

FORT WORDEN STATE PARK, Port Townsend, WA 98368; (206) 385-4370. Located one mile north of Port Townsend.

Open on a seasonal basis; contact the park for information.

(Courtesy Washington State Parks and Recreation Commission)

PORT TOWNSEND

HASTINGS HOUSE
1889

Frank Hastings, son of Port Townsend's founder and a prominent businessman, began building his brick, clapboard, and shingle Queen Anne house in 1889. Plans called for an elegant interior costing some $10,000, but Hastings, financially embarrassed by the depression in the following year, was forced to move into an uncompleted home. Hastings House remained unfinished until C. A. Olsen purchased the property—residence, carriage house and six lots—in 1904 for $2,500.

Hastings House is now a bed and breakfast inn, open for tours every afternoon year round. It is regarded as an excellent example of the Queen Anne style, popular with architects and photographers for its asymmetrical towers and turrets. Its interior boasts a massive ground-floor staircase installed by Olsen; it was the first home in Port Townsend to have electricity.

HASTINGS HOUSE, 313 Walker Street, Port Townsend, WA 09368; (206) 385-3553.
Tour hours: 12–4:30 daily.
Admission fee.
(Courtesy Mrs. Grace Pierson)

PORT TOWNSEND

ROTHSCHILD HOUSE
1868

"Just enough to get the name, not the money" was the way D. C. H. Rothschild described his relationship to the princely European bankers. Nevertheless, he did quite well for himself with mercantile stores in California and Bellingham and with the general store he opened in Port Townsend in 1858. Five years later he married Dorette Hartung, a girl still in her teens; their first three children were born in the apartment above the Port Townsend store. In 1868 Rothschild began building this eight-room frame house, which remained in the Rothschild family for nearly a century.

Rothschild House is shown with most of the original furnishings and decoration. As a consequence, it conveys an unusually evocative image of family life at the end of the nineteenth century. Visitors with a fondness for old gardens should take a turn around the grounds. The herb garden has been restored, and the flower garden boasts many old varieties of lilacs, peonies, and roses.

ROTHSCHILD HOUSE, Franklin and Taylor streets, Port Townsend, WA 98368.
Hours: Mid-May–mid-September, 10–6 daily.
(Courtesy State of Washington Parks and Recreation Department)

PORT TOWNSEND

STARRETT HOUSE
1889

George E. Starrett, a leading contractor and mill owner who came to Port Townsend in 1885, built this striking Queen Anne/Stick-style residence as his home. Fine woodwork characterized the interior—bannisters and newel posts for the free-hung staircase in the entrance hall were carved from five different kinds of wood. The decoration is rich, and restoration has uncovered frescoes in the dining and music rooms as well as the well-known Four Seasons series painted by Otto Chapman on the tower ceiling. Starrett House today is a bed and breakfast inn; visitors are welcome to tour the premises during the afternoon.

STARRETT HOUSE, 744 Clay Street, Port Townsend, WA 98368; (206) 385-2976.
Hours: 12–4 daily.
Admission fee.
(Courtesy Susan and Richard Thompson)

PUYALLUP

MEEKER MANSION
1890

Eclectic in style, the seventeen-room late-Victorian mansion built by pioneer hop farmer and entrepreneur Ezra Meeker features a widow's walk encircling the roof, ceilings painted in floral and geometric designs, stained-glass windows, ornately carved interior woodwork, and a ballroom on the third floor. For a man who had arrived in Puyallup too poor even to own an overcoat, the house was a triumphant statement. It has been refurbished in the 1890s style and contains a few original Meeker items.

Meeker devoted the last twenty years of his long life to marking the Oregon Trail, which he and his wife had followed in 1852. To dramatize his project Meeker crossed the continent by ox team and wagon at the age of seventy-six and again at age eighty; at ninety-four he flew the route in an airplane. He died in Seattle in 1928, two years short of a century.

MEEKER MANSION, 321 East Pioneer Avenue,
Puyallup, WA 98371; (206) 848-1770.
Hours: 1–4 Wednesday–Sunday.
Admission by donation.
(Courtesy Ezra Meeker Historical Society, Inc.)

REDMOND

MARYMOOR MUSEUM (James W. Clise House) 1904–07

James W. Clise, a prosperous Seattle banker and president of the state's first trust company, built a hunting lodge at the Marymoor site in 1904. By 1907 he had expanded the lodge into a twenty-eight-room, two-story Tudoresque mansion surrounded by 350 acres, which he developed into a showcase farm famous for its Ayreshire cattle and Morgan horses. Willowmoor was also known for its extensive gardens, supervised by an English gardener who imported many plants from Europe and the Orient and who thought nothing of training several hundred roses on the huge pergola near the house.

The Clises also owned homes in Seattle and in California, and in 1928 they decided to sell Willowmoor. Slightly altered by subsequent owners, the mansion was purchased by King County in 1963; ten rooms in the north wing now compose the Marymoor Museum, which retains a few items once owned by the Clises. The park, expanded recently to five hundred acres, includes two important prehistoric Indian sites on the banks of the Sammamish River.

MARYMOOR MUSEUM, Marymoor County Park (off Lake Sammamish Parkway N.E., Highway 901), Redmond, WA 98052; (206) 885-3684.
Hours: June–Labor Day, 10–2 Tuesday, 1–5 Saturday–Sunday; Labor Day–May, 10–2 Tuesday, 1–4 Sunday.
(Courtesy Marymoor Museum)

RITZVILLE

DR. FRANK R. BURROUGHS MUSEUM 1889

Local lore has it that Dr. Frank R. Burroughs was on his way to Seattle when he stopped in Ritzville to visit relatives and was pressed into remaining a lifetime as the town's physician. The eclectic two-story home he built for his family was remodeled in 1903. Although under restoration, an appointment may be made to view the interior, which retains much of its original decor as well as the doctor's records and equipment. The screen behind which the Burroughs' maid would wait in the dining room, iron bedsteads with brass knobs, handsomely decorated trunks, and family photographs are among the family possessions that remain to conjure a portrait of the family and professional life of a country doctor in the horse and buggy age.

DR. FRANK R. BURROUGHS MUSEUM, 408 West Main Street, Ritzville, WA 99169.
Admission by appointment only. Call the City Clerk's office, (509) 659-1930.
(Courtesy Dr. Frank R. Burroughs Museum)

HISTORICAL HOME
Dr. Frank R. Burroughs MUSEUM

SEATTLE

DIOCESAN HOUSE
(Eliza Ferry Leary House)
1903

On a hill overlooking Lake Union is the stone mansion that financier John Leary and his second wife, Eliza Ferry Leary, intended to be the most beautiful residence in Seattle. Designed by architects John Graham and Arthur Bodley, it supposedly was patterned on an Irish manor house visited by the Learys. The richly finished interior is notable for its plasterwork, heraldic decoration, marble fireplaces, and handcarved woodwork. There is a smoking room where gold leaf has been applied to the walls and a painted frieze circumscribes the top, and a dining room paneled in choice mahogany. But the outstanding feature is the vaulted baronial hall paneled with Circassian walnut. Exquisitely crafted and embellished, the manufacture of the paneling occupied several Belgian craftsmen for four years.

The house was not finished when John Leary died in California in 1905; Mrs. Leary completed it as she felt he would have liked it and resided there until her death. In World War II Leary House was donated to the Red Cross. It now serves as the offices of the Episcopal diocese of Olympia.

DIOCESAN HOUSE (Eliza Ferry Leary House), 1551 Tenth Avenue E, Seattle, WA 98102; (206) 325-4200.
Hours: 9–5 Monday–Friday, by appointment only. Apply to the archivist.
(Courtesy Diocese of Olympia)

SEATTLE

STIMSON-GREEN MANSION
1901

The Stimson-Green Mansion is a half-timbered Tudor-style residence designed by one of Washington's leading architects, Kirtland K. Cutter, for the wealthy lumberman C. D. Stimson. In 1914 it was sold to Joshua Green, a banker and president of the Puget Sound Navigation Company, whose family lived there until 1975. The finely carved paneling of imported hardwoods is notable, as is the drawing room's massive Gothic fireplace with hand-carved oak lions on each side.

STIMSON-GREEN MANSION, 1204 Minor Avenue, Seattle, WA 98101; (206) 624-0474.
Open for tour groups of 15 or more only, by appointment.
Admission fee.
(Courtesy Cleveland and Associates Advertising Agency)

SNOHOMISH

BLACKMAN MUSEUM 1878

Three Blackman brothers, who came West in 1872, were among the first to settle Snohomish. Sons of a Maine woodsman, the brothers began a logging operation in 1875 at Blackman's Lake, and Alanson, the eldest, and his brother Elhanan revolutionized the logging industry by developing a famous logging truck and tripper shingle machine. They built their first mill on the Snohomish River in 1883. Hyrcanus, the youngest brother, became the firm's accountant and eventually Snohomish's first mayor. It was he who built the Queen Anne–style house which now serves as a local museum. Most of the interior furnishings are original to the house, as is the entry stairwell wallpaper, applied more than a century ago. Other period furnishings have been donated by Snohomish area residents.

BLACKMAN MUSEUM, 118 Avenue A, Snohomish, WA 98290.
Hours: 12–4 Saturday and Sunday.
(Courtesy Snohomish Historical Society)

SPOKANE

GRACE CAMPBELL MEMORIAL HOUSE 1898
Cheney Cowles Memorial Museum

After accumulating a fortune in the gold mines of the Coeur d'Alenes and British Columbia, Amasa B. Campbell commissioned the prominent architect Kirtland K. Cutter to design a mansion on this site above the Spokane River in the fashionable Brown's Addition section. Cutter thoroughly understood the implicit requirements of his millionaire clients for residences appropriate to their affluence and position in society. Accordingly, he designed a spacious nineteen-room mansion in the Tudoresque style with a richly embellished interior to complement the Campbells' lifestyle. Room decor ranged from the rococo elegance of Mrs. Campbell's Louis XV reception room to the snugly informal basement card room, the only place in the house where gentlemen were permitted to smoke. Cutter also provided interior decorating services, and many of the furnishings were his selections.

Campbell House was donated to the Eastern Washington Historical Society by the owners' only child, Helen Campbell Powell, as a memorial to her mother. In planning restoration of the house the historical society had access to Cutter's original cost inventory. Now fully restored and with a few original furnishings intact, the house serves as a monument to Spokane's "Age of Elegance." An enclosed walkway links Campbell House to the Cheney Cowles Memorial Museum next door, which contains historical and natural-history exhibits and an art gallery.

GRACE CAMPBELL MEMORIAL HOUSE, West 2316 First Avenue, Spokane, WA 99204; (509) 456-3931.
Hours: 10–4 Tuesday–Saturday; 2–5 Sunday.
(Courtesy Eastern Washington Historical Society)

SPOKANE

PATSY CLARK'S
(Patrick F. Clark House)
1895–98

Overlooking Coeur d'Alene Park in the historic Brown's Addition district is one of the most opulent homes ever built in the Pacific Northwest.

Patrick F. Clark, an Irish immigrant who made his millions in the mines of Montana, British Columbia, and Idaho, commissioned architect Kirtland K. Cutter to design for him the most luxurious residence in Spokane using nothing but the best materials, regardless of cost. Cutter achieved a boldly eclectic mansion with twenty-six rooms where Roman, French, Chinese, Egyptian, and Moorish elements blend with rich effect. There is much for the devotee of superb craftsmanship and materials here.

Cutter found the sepia sandstone for the exterior trim in Italy; the bricks were made in St. Louis; the column caps were hand-sculpted in Italy; Tiffany crafted windows and a clock. In the Mooresque foyer, itself paneled in oak overlaid with leather, the eye is led immediately to a Tiffany window of some four thousand pieces of stained glass suggesting peacock tailfeathers, and to the large black-oak Tiffany grandfather clock. The spacious reception rooms (each different) provided the settings the affable magnate considered appropriate for entertaining his friends, among them Marcus Daly and John D. Rockefeller. The simple servants' quarters markedly underscore the social distinctions of the age.

"Patsy" Clark died in 1915 and his widow sold the house in 1926. Today, sympathetically adapted, it is a restaurant called, appropriately enough, Patsy Clark's. Two-thirds of the original furnishings have been returned to the house, and three rooms on the second floor are maintained much as the Clark family would have known them. Visitors are welcome at Patsy Clark's. Those who do not choose to take a meal are asked to come after 3 P.M.

PATSY CLARK'S, West 2208 Second Avenue, Spokane, WA 99204; (509) 838-8300.
Open daily during restaurant hours or after 3 P.M.
(Courtesy Patsy Clark's Restaurant)

SPOKANE

GLOVER HOUSE
1888

Kirtland K. Cutter's design for this twenty-two-room half-timbered baronial mansion is said to have established his architectural reputation among Spokane's gold millionaires at the turn of the century. His client was James N. Glover, the "Father of Spokane," who had come to the Spokane River valley in 1873 with the dream of building a city in the wilderness. He developed Spokane's first sawmill, established the first store, opened the first bank, platted the town, named the streets, and served as mayor in 1884.

Glover and Spokane prospered during the boom years of the eighties, but in 1895 he suffered heavy financial losses and was ultimately forced to sell the house. Now the activities center and offices of the Unitarian Church, it retains some furnishings that evoke the opulent era of the Glovers. Particularly impressive is the two-story living room and ballroom with its gallery, grand staircase, and painted silk ceiling.

GLOVER HOUSE, West 321 Eighth Avenue,
Spokane, WA 99204; (509) 624-4802.
Open daily during office hours.
(Courtesy Unitarian Church; The Glover House Foundation)

STEILACOOM

NATHANIEL ORR HOUSE AND PIONEER ORCHARD 1853–57

In 1853 Nathaniel Hope Orr, a Virginian of Scottish descent, began building this attractive wood-frame house in a simplified version of the Greek Revival style. When completed in 1857 it boasted bachelor's quarters upstairs and a wagon shop downstairs where Orr turned out a variety of wood products. Family history has it that he operated the first powered lathe in the area in this shop. It was turned by an ingenious contraption linking a patient old horse in the yard to the lathe by means of a pole passed through a hole knocked in the wall. Orr was also an orchardist and a merchant, establishing in partnership with Philip Keach Steilacoom's merchandise store a commercial orchard that supplied much of the area's orchard stock.

The Orr House is a rare opportunity to visit a Northwest home occupied by one family for more than a century. The last Orr to live there was Nathaniel's son Glenn, who died in 1974 at the age of ninety-three. The house was substantially altered only once—when Nathaniel married Emma Thompson of Victoria in 1868 and converted his workshop into the parlor, bedroom, sitting room, and kitchen you see today. Almost all the furnishings are Orr originals. Emma brought the Empire bedroom set and the horsehair sofa and chairs in the front parlor from Victoria as wedding gifts. Orr made most of the other furniture, even upholstering the sofas. Fruit trees that he planted still grow in the orchard that adjoins the house.

NATHANIEL ORR HOUSE AND PIONEER ORCHARD,
1811 Rainier Street, Steilacoom, WA 98388;
(206) 588-8115 or 584-8623.

Hours: April–October, 1–4 Sunday. Special tours may be arranged at any time of the year.

Admission fee.

(Courtesy Steilacoom Historical Museum Association)

1811

SUMNER

SUMNER RYAN HOUSE MUSEUM
1875; enlarged 1885

The home of Sumner's first mayor, George Ryan, is a two-story Classical Revival farmhouse with Gothic Revival detail and a spindle-trimmed porch that was added in the 1880s. It incorporates an earlier structure, a three-room cabin built in 1875 for Ryan and his future wife Lucy V. Wood by two friends, while Ryan earned the cost of materials as a bookkeeper at the Port Gamble sawmill. After his marriage Ryan operated a hop farm while his wife ran the local post office in the little house; later he was a founding partner of a large sawmill two miles northeast of Sumner. Old-timers never forgot the thunder of the logs as they shot down a greased chute to his millpond.

In 1926 his descendants gave the Ryan home to the city of Sumner to use as its library. Now a museum, the house is being restored to its appearance in the 1890s and features changing displays of local history. Some of the trees planted by Lucy Ryan in 1876 still grow in the gardens that surround the house.

SUMNER RYAN HOUSE MUSEUM, 1228 Main Street,
Sumner, WA 98390; (206) 863-5567.
Hours: April–August, 1–5 Saturday and Sunday.
Admission by donation.
(Courtesy Sumner Historical Society)

TACOMA

FORT NISQUALLY FACTOR'S HOUSE
Ca. 1853

Built about 1853 by the Hudson's Bay Company for their supply and communication center at old Fort Nisqually, the Factor's House now stands in Tacoma's Point Defiance Park in a reconstruction of the fort. The house follows the Company's traditional building style, with a clapboard exterior and a shingle roof setting it apart from the ruder structures in the compound. The five ground-floor rooms were used both for family and business activities; the upper story probably served as the children's bedroom. In its heyday many prominent visitors were entertained in the house, among them Isaac Stevens, first governor of Washington Territory.

Today the Factor's House is a museum depicting the history of the Hudson's Bay Company in the Pacific Northwest. Other structures in the compound are reconstructions, built from surviving records to resemble Fort Nisqually's appearance in 1843 as closely as possible.

FORT NISQUALLY FACTOR'S HOUSE, Point Defiance Park, Tacoma, WA 98407; (206) 759-1246.
Hours: Memorial Day–Labor Day, 12–6; rest of year, 1–4 Wednesday–Sunday. Tours by appointment.
(Courtesy Metropolitan Park District)

TUMWATER

CROSBY HOUSE
1858

This charming little house at the foot of Tumwater Falls has changed little since Nathaniel Crosby III built it for his bride, Cordelia Jane Smith Crosby, in 1858. Of wood-frame construction, it combines Greek and Gothic Revival elements and retains all its original ornate exterior wood carvings.

Crosby was only thirteen when he arrived in Portland, Oregon, aboard the brig *Grecian*. Earlier his father, Capt. Nathaniel Crosby, Jr., had sailed around the Horn with supplies for the early settlers; impressed by the prospects, he then persuaded the entire Crosby clan to leave their homes in Wiscasset, Maine, and settle in the Northwest. Some chose to stay in Astoria. Crosby's family was among those who continued to Olympia (then known as New Market), where they are believed to have built a general store. His uncle Clanrick bought the area's only sawmill and a gristmill.

After Crosby and his family left Tumwater, the house passed through many hands before its acquisition by the Daughters of the Pioneers. Today it is furnished almost entirely with antiques of the Civil War period donated by descendants of pioneers who settled western Washington before 1860. In the yard there still are cherry trees that Crosby planted.

CROSBY HOUSE, 708 Deschutes Way, Tumwater, WA 98501.
Hours: Varying. Direct inquiries to Henderson House Pictorial Museum, (206) 753-8583.
(Courtesy Daughters of the Pioneers of Washington, Olympia Chapter 4)

TUMWATER

HENDERSON HOUSE
1905

Recently restored by the City of Tumwater to its original condition, Henderson House is a two-story Carpenter Gothic residence that has been occupied by several families over the years. The house now serves as a pictorial museum featuring the history of life along the Deschutes River. There are period furnishings, and the interior fixtures of Tumwater's original post office, postal boxes and all, have been incorporated. Beside the house is a replica of a log cabin, furnished with pioneer artifacts.

HENDERSON HOUSE, 602 North Deschutes Way, Tumwater, WA 98501; (206) 753-8583.
Hours: Summer, 11:30–3:30 Monday–Friday; 1–5 weekends and holidays.
(Courtesy Henderson House Pictorial Museum)

VANCOUVER

COVINGTON HOUSE
1846

Richard Covington, builder of this simple log house, was an English employee of the Hudson's Bay Company at Fort Vancouver. Since Covington and his wife were of a hospitable disposition and possessed the first piano brought to Washington Territory, their home became the center of the area's social life. They also operated a boarding school for children in the house until 1862. The house was originally located on Covington's land grant in the Orchards area about five miles east of Vancouver. It was moved log by log to its present site in 1926.

COVINGTON HOUSE, 4303 Main Street,
Vancouver, WA 98660; (206) 693-6825.
Located opposite State Highway Department building.
Hours: June–August, 10–4, Tuesday and Thursday.
Admission by donation.
(Courtesy Vancouver Woman's Club)

VANCOUVER

ULYSSES S. GRANT MUSEUM
1849

One of two large log houses built by the army in 1849, Grant House was the building used as offices by Lt. Ulysses S. Grant when he came to Fort Vancouver in 1852 as regimental quartermaster of the Fourth Infantry. Other distinguished officers who used the building either as living quarters or as a quartermaster building were William T. Sherman, Winfield S. Scott, and George Marshall, who became U.S. Army chief of staff during World War II. It is now a historical museum and displays furniture once owned by Grant.

ULYSSES S. GRANT MUSEUM, 1106 East Evergreen Boulevard, Vancouver, WA 98661; (206) 693-9743.
Hours: 1–4 Monday–Wednesday; 1–5 Friday–Sunday.
Admission fee.
(Courtesy Soroptimist International of Vancouver, Inc.)

VANCOUVER

CHARLES W. SLOCUM HOUSE
1867

This handsome Italianate villa was built by Edward Slocum for his brother Charles, a leading Vancouver merchant, to the pattern of their family home in Rhode Island. It was one of Vancouver's first really elegant residences (Edward also built homes for himself and his cousin William Hazard), with a handsome curving stairway of rosewood and Honduras mahogany, decorative plaster ceilings with chandeliers suspended from cast-plaster medallions, raised panel doors, and a carved marble fireplace. When threatened with demolition in the 1960s, the house was moved to its present site in Esther Short Park. It now serves as a community theater and concert hall.

CHARLES W. SLOCUM HOUSE, 605 Esther Street, Vancouver, WA 98660.
Access at theatre performances. Group tours by appointment. Call Vancouver Parks and Recreation Department, (206) 696-8171.
(Courtesy Old Slocum House Theatre Company)

Slocum
House

WAITSBURG

BRUCE MEMORIAL MUSEUM
1883

This simplified Italianate mansion shaded by firs was the home of a successful pioneer farmer, merchant, and land dealer, William Perry Bruce, and his wife Caroline O'Neal Bruce.

Early Waitsburg owed much to this public-spirited couple. Natives of Indiana, they arrived in the Touchet Valley in 1861 after farming in Oregon for nine years, and in the following year Bruce acquired the Isaac Levens claim on which most of Waitsburg now stands. In 1863 he donated part of his claim for the area's first business, Wait's Mill. After platting and surveying the town in 1868, he gave liberally to many civic enterprises. Among his gifts were land and money for a school and a bridge.

The Bruce mansion remained in the family until 1921. For a period it served as the town's library. After years of neglect, it was acquired in 1971 by the Waitsburg Historical Society and restored as closely as possible to its original appearance. Some of the millwork is thought to have been shipped from India, Bruce's birthplace. Today it preserves heirlooms of Touchet Valley pioneers, among them three pieces of Bruce's furniture.

BRUCE MEMORIAL MUSEUM, 318 Main Street, Waitsburg, WA 99361.
Open by appointment. Call (509) 337-6287 or 337-6631.
(Courtesy Waitsburg Historical Society)

WALLA WALLA

FORT WALLA WALLA MUSEUM COMPLEX PIONEER VILLAGE

Several buildings typical of the Walla Walla Valley's early vernacular architecture have been relocated here to simulate a typical pioneer-era community. There is a railway depot dating from about 1880; a country store; a blacksmith shop; a barber's shop and a doctor's office; the old Prescott jail; and one of the best-preserved one-room school houses in the area, as well as three pioneer cabins. On the slope overlooking the village a group of modern buildings houses the museum's agricultural history displays, among them a combine harnessed to thirty-three fiberglass mules by a Shenandoah hitch, a device that enabled one man to control the entire team.

Ransom Clark Cabin

1859

This four-room log cabin begun by Ransom Clark, who had been a member of Lt. John Fremont's 1843 surveying expedition, formerly stood on Clark's land grant about a mile south of Walla Walla. Clark had farmed in Yamhill County, operated a hotel in Portland, and tried his luck gold mining in California and Canada before he decided to settle in the Walla Walla Valley in 1855. Due to Indian uprisings which temporarily forced all settlers out of the valley, Clark died before the cabin was completed, but his widow Lettice and their children moved into the unfinished cabin in order to prove the claim.

The cabin is unusual: a breezeway separates the two living rooms; nailed to one wall is a perpendicular ladder by which the children climbed to bed. Simple period furnishings effectively convey a sense of life in the 1860s. Among them are a leather-bound trunk brought from San Francisco in 1858 by Almos Reynolds, Mrs. Clark's second husband, and a spinning wheel and an apple-butter jar that came across the plains with Mrs. Clark's family.

FORT WALLA WALLA MUSEUM COMPLEX, Ransom Clark Cabin, The Dalles Military Road, Walla Walla, WA 99362; (509) 525-7703.
Hours: May, June, and September, 1–5 Saturday –Sunday and holidays; July–August, Tuesday–Sunday.
Admission fee.
(Courtesy Walla Walla Valley Pioneer and Historical Society)

WALLA WALLA

KIRKMAN HOUSE MUSEUM
1880

William Kirkman, builder of this roseate brick mansion in the Italianate style, was an Englishman who made his fortune in the cattle-raising and meat-packing businesses, after an adventurous youth that took him as far afield as Australia, the Hawaiian Islands, Canada, and the California goldfields. The house remained in the Kirkman family until 1919, when his widow Isabella gave it to Walla Walla College to establish a William Kirkman chair in history; it was used as a dormitory until the college sold the property in the 1920s. During that time one of the occupants was Walter Brattain, later a Nobel prizewinner for his work in developing the transistor.

Kirkman House is now being restored to its former dignity after a long period as an apartment house. At present the major reception rooms, two bedrooms, and the sewing room are shown, furnished with period antiques to approximate their appearance when the Kirkmans lived there. Of particular interest are the hand-painted *faux marbre* walls in the hallway, which carry up to the third floor; the handsome parquet floors using maple, walnut, and oak, and some ornate brass hardware. In the garden the former carriage house is now Cherry Street Collectibles, the museum shop selling antiques and collectibles to help defray restoration costs.

KIRKMAN HOUSE MUSEUM, 214 North Colville Street, Walla Walla, WA 99362; (509) 529-4373.
Hours: 1–4:30 weekdays or by appointment.
Admission fee.
(Courtesy Historical Architecture Development Corporation)

WHITE SWAN

FORT SIMCOE STATE HISTORIC PARK
1856–59

Fort Simcoe was one of two army posts established in the interior of Washington in response to Indian uprisings that began in the fall of 1855. The site was both strategic and symbolic, occupying an ancient gathering place of the Yakima Indians at the intersection of many trails. The army did not remain long at Fort Simcoe, however. In 1859 the fort was turned over to the Department of Indian Affairs and served as an Indian agency and as a school before its acquisition as a state historic park. Only five buildings remain of the military structures that formerly lined the parade ground. The commanding officer's house is particularly noteworthy. Designed in the Gothic Revival style by Louis Scholl, an army draftsman-architect at Fort Dalles, it has been restored and refurnished to the period of U.S. Army occupancy.

FORT SIMCOE STATE HISTORIC PARK, Fort Road, White Swan (near Yakima), WA 98952; (509) 874-2372.
Hours: May–October, 8–5 daily.
(Courtesy Washington State Parks and Recreation Commission)

YACOLT

POMEROY HOUSE
1915

Pomeroy House, oldest in the Lucia Falls area, was built by E. C. Pomeroy in 1915. A Canadian of English descent, Pomeroy came to the area in 1910 and established a farm for his wife and five children.

The present house replaced an earlier structure built in 1910 and destroyed by a forest fire. Logs for the first story were felled on the site; other boards came from old mill buildings in the area. Many of the moldings are the work of Pomeroy and his son Thomas. The living room retains the brick fireplace of the first home.

Pomeroy House today is occupied by descendants who are restoring both the house and its acreage as a turn-of-the-century working farm. Many of the original plantings still grow in the garden; the herbs once cultivated by the first Mrs. Pomeroy are being replanted. The former carriage house is now a gift shop; a blacksmith shop stands nearby. The smithy, originally a mill house and for a time the valley's first schoolhouse, holds Pomeroy's tools, now used in demonstrations of the blacksmith's craft.

POMEROY HOUSE, 10902 Northeast Lucia Falls Road, Yacolt, WA 98675; (206) 686-3637 or 694-5294.

Hours: House open by appointment and during National Historical Preservation Week. Gift shop open daily, 10–5 Monday–Saturday; 1–5 Sunday.

(Courtesy Mrs. Lillian Freese)

INDEX